# THE MEASURE OF GREATNESS

An Inquiry Into the
Unique Traits and
Talents That Set Certain
Athletes Apart From
the Rest of the Field

PARTON KEESE

Prentice-Hall, Inc.          Englewood Cliffs, New Jersey

The Measure of Greatness by Parton Keese
Copyright © 1981 by Parton Keese
Chapters 1, 5, 6, 7, 9, and 10 adapted from material which originally
appeared in The New York Times.
© 1976 by the New York Times Company. Reprinted by permission.

All rights reserved. No part of this book may be
reproduced in any form or by any means, except
for the inclusion of brief quotations in a review,
without permission in writing from the publisher.
Address inquiries to Prentice-Hall, Inc., Englewood
Cliffs, N.J. 07632

Printed in the United States of America

Prentice-Hall International, Inc., London
Prentice-Hall of Australia, Pty. Ltd., Sydney
Prentice-Hall of Canada, Ltd., Toronto
Prentice-Hall of India Private Ltd., New Delhi
Prentice-Hall of Japan, Inc., Tokyo
Prentice-Hall of Southeast Asia Pte. Ltd., Singapore
Whitehall Books Limited, Wellington, New Zealand

10 9 8 7 6 5 4 3 2 1

**Library of Congress Cataloging in Publication Data**

Keese, Parton.
    The measure of greatness.

    SUMMARY: Discusses 12 leading athletes from
several major sports in an attempt to isolate the
particular quality that has made each one
outstanding.
    1. Athletes—Biography—Juvenile literature.
[1. Athletes]  I. Title.
GV697.A1K38    796'.092'2  [B]  [920]  80-17027
ISBN 0-13-567800-5

Photo Credits

Pages 1 and 2
Courtesy of Robert L. Smith Photography, Elma, N.Y.
Pages 29 and 30
Courtesy of the California Angels
Pages 69, 70, 149, and 150
Courtesy of TENNIS magazine

KENNEDY

81   5742

# CONTENTS

# ACKNOWLEDGEMENTS

Without the inspiration, knowledge, and help of the following persons, this book could not have been written: James Tuite, Joseph Durso, Gerald Eskenazi, Sam Goldaper, Alex Yannis, Eleanor Rawson, and Jacques deSpoelbergh.

# INTRODUCTION

Did you ever wonder why, out of the thousands of athletes who compete in all the various sports, one or two usually climb to the top of the heap and stay there for a long time exerting their superiority over the rest? In most cases, they possess similar physical qualities, have practiced the same long hours perfecting their skills and can jump, throw, run, and think with seemingly identical ability. If they were all together in a gym or on a field doing their thing, could you point to one or two and say with any certainty: "That one, he'll be the best" or "She stands out above everyone else"?

You might even go about it more scientifically, measuring size, speed, and strength, giving tests in intelligence, aptitude, and achievement, or having every athlete demonstrate individually on a machine or computer just how coordinated and talented he or she is. But then, when the game commences, and you've made your choices, you inevitably are fooled. The smaller athlete defeats the bigger one; the slower performer beats a quicker one, and a technically perfect participant loses out to a more awkward one.

They all work in a world of tangible goals, 100-yard fields, 90-foot basepaths, equal-sized courts, etc. They use identical equipment, the same ball, puck, or glove. Some are very tall, like Kareem Abdul-Jabbar, but there are taller basketball players. Some are very fast, like O. J. Simpson, but there are even faster men. Some are women, like Billie Jean King, with damaged knees and weak eyes. Some are just average-sized men, like Tom Seaver, Jimmy Connors, and Bobby Orr. But somehow, because of something extra, some rise to the top, becoming superstars in an industry dominated by stars.

This book is an attempt to answer intriguing questions such as: What made Pele the world's greatest soccer player and Muhammad Ali the best prizefighter? What motivates a Julius Erving into possessing basketball's most startling moves? How did Rod Carew win seven batting titles? What secret ingredient allows Jack Nicklaus to be called the finest golfer ever?

These athletes tower over their rivals, who, on the surface, seem as aptly endowed. Yet, when the season's statistics are engraved for posterity, the sober facts remain: One pitcher strikes out 200 batters every summer; one running back gains 2,000 yards in the fall; one skater scores 65 goals each winter, setting standards in artistry and take-home pay.

To achieve the true perspective on this phenomenon, the superathletes themselves were approached and asked to reflect on their own artistry. Their colleagues were questioned, too, as were their coaches, families, friends, and rivals, to see if they held the secrets of the forces that determine what brings ultimate success. When the pieces of all the puzzles were put together, they not only became fascinating reading, but also indicated that the styles, techniques, gamesmanship, and tools of the trade that so impress and astonish the public made our dozen selections as different as piano prodigies are from each other.

It is also interesting to note at this time which superstars were even aware of the reasons that had catapulted them to the pinnacles of their sport, which ones were honestly surprised at how they got where they are, which ones were, perhaps, too modest to reveal very much about themselves, and which ones, for one reason or another, either tried to hide the truth or tried to cloud reality with hyperbole.

In the first category, you could place Tom Seaver, O. J. Simpson, Phil Esposito, and Billie Jean King, all of whom had obviously thought deeply about their accomplishments long before this book was planned. Their introspective natures made chapters on them the easiest and most natural.

Unable to explain their superiority satisfactorily (thus causing outside sources to be used) were Bobby Orr (who never really liked to talk about himself and could be classified as too modest as well); Jack Nicklaus (who tried but could not match those around him who knew him better than he did himself); and Pele, a lovable character who also can't help equivocating.

The "shy" or "too busy" list includes Rod Carew and Kareem Abdul-Jabbar, who might have been approached at the wrong time in their hectic careers, while those who will probably deny vehemently the conclusions drawn here are Jimmy Connors, Ali, and Julius Erving, who seems to be saving such introspection for his autobiography. Ali, of course, can change his mind as fast as his mouth allows, while the once-irascible Connors may not care less now that he is married and a father.

What any writer fears the most, however, is what can happen to his subjects between the time the information is reported to the date the work is actually published. There are young sports freaks, for instance, who have never heard of Tommy Henrich, Jon Arnett, George Mikan, Byron Nelson, Andy Bathgate, Pancho Segura or Hammerin' Henry Armstrong, all heroes who have passed in the night. The fear is that one or more of the twelve written about here will go downhill overnight and lose credibility.

It does me proud, as they say, to note the comebacks of Billie Jean King, Tom Seaver, Phil Esposito, Julius Erving, Jimmy Connors, and even Ali (who may never give up), just when their careers had seemingly taken a turn toward oblivion. Their refusal to say die proves the very theme of the book: There is something unique in each of these superhumans, and whatever the special elements of his or her psyche, it sets him or her apart from other stars and creates that singular status of its own.

Call it what you will; I call it The Measure of Greatness.

# O.J. SIMPSON

## An Optical Illusion
## with a Football

He could run the hundred in 9.4 seconds, faster than nearly any other running back in football. He stood 6 feet 1 inch and weighed 207 pounds, bigger than the other speed merchants of the National Football League. He could stop like a door slamming, then regain his lightning pace instantly, which put him in the realm of the shiftiest ballcarriers ever seen. Besides that, he had the resolute will to succeed that only those who have grown up in the ghetto can understand.

To opposing players, especially, he looked like an optical illusion.

But as formidable and unparalleled as those credentials might seem, they do not include the single unique quality that transformed O.J. Simpson from just a sensational player into the exclusive club reserved for the elite. The opposition thought it knew what it was. O.J.'s coaches marveled at it. His teammates shook their heads and were just glad he was on their side.

What was Simpson's secret ingredient?

One trainer labeled it in his own terms: "kinesthetic awareness." In other words, explained the trainer, O.J. knows where he is in relation to his body and what his body must do.

The N.F.L. put it more simply and called Simpson's gift "pure E.S.P." But though Simpson admitted to having "a certain amount of extrasensory perception," he himself did not credit E.S.P. entirely for his record-smashing assault on pro football.

"Simpson is in a different category from any runner who played this game," said one defensive coach, all too familiar with trying to stop O.J. Having spent the major part of his coaching season attempting to devise defenses to contain the runner, he knew what he was talking about.

The record, of course, speaks the loudest, though we need only touch upon the cream of the cream: "Orenthal James Simpson: only N.F.L. runner to total over 2,000 yards rushing in one season. Also holds record for most touchdowns, one year, with 23." The rest of the raves include words like "fastest," "most elusive," "most powerful," "electrifying," etc.

These are outstanding figures, the kind of numbers that wow the brain and numb logical thinking processes. But still, they don't explain the mystical formula of O.J. Simpson, and to be truthful, even he is unsure of the reason, since it has been a natural part of him rather than something developed or acquired. Yet, the explanations hit closer and closer the more they are analyzed as one.

O.J. likes to say, "I have a feeling for where everybody on a football field is."

That's nice to have, all right, but for Eddie Abramoski, the trainer of the Buffalo Bills, where Simpson performed most of his magic, it was something different. "O.J. is bow-legged. That's the reality. And it gives him outstanding balance."

O.J. thinks that one over for an instant and replies: "Yes, that may present some type of optical illusion to my opponents. I look funny, and they don't know where to grab me."

For all his so-called funny looks, Simpson really possesses a combination of extraordinary traits—including physical, mental, and emotional— if someone were trying to create the perfect football player, he would probably end up with another O.J. Simpson.

Think of what a running back in professional football must be able to accomplish, as well as withstand: If he carries 20 or more times, he must endure 20 or more tackles by all kinds of players, many of whom weigh over 250 pounds.

Then he must be quick enough to pierce through a small opening in the line and escape from all these 250-pound-and-over behemoths out to destroy him. Next in order come the hell-bent linebackers, a group who mix agility with ferocity and size. Runners breaking through the lines collide with these blocks of granite; the great ones bounce off.

Finally, the runner meets up with the secondary, de-

4

fensive backs as fast or faster than he is. This is where they separate the superstars from the regular stars, the O.J.'s from the Almosts.

"Our offense is geared to get me into the secondary," Simpson said of his Buffalo team. "Much of my success when I get past the line of scrimmage is based on two factors: One, I'm usually faster than the secondary; and two, I'm usually bigger than they are."

Faster and bigger, quicker and more agile. Said Abramoski: "Look at O.J. and you might be fooled. He doesn't look 207. More like 190, maybe. You see, he's so well-proportioned. His muscles are well-defined too.

"And he can run as fast in a football uniform as out of one. We had the Big Ten dash champion on our team once. He could run a 9.3 in the 100, faster than O.J., but he couldn't run in a uniform. Do you remember that Superstars competition on television where O.J. ran the 100 in 9.6—in sneakers?"

Now we're back to that other elusive quality, E.S.P., or kinesthetic awareness, or optical illusion, or whatever. Forget the name, ponder on what it can do. With this attribute, Simpson can change plans even while an enemy linebacker is sailing in on him alone.

Against the Jets one day, Simpson ran for 244 yards on 32 carries, not around end, not on screen passes and flanker pitchouts, but up the middle, over the guards, through the line. The Jets knew where he was going to go and they had planned accordingly. Except for 70 yards called back because of Buffalo penalties, the defense failed absolutely to stop O.J.

"Do you realize that 90 percent of O.J.'s yardage through our line," said the Jets' defensive coach, "was made through secondary holes. We had the primary holes sewed up. But he is unique. His forte is waiting and watching. He doesn't always go to the predetermined path. He bounces, literally and figuratively."

This then is the scene in slow-motion if you are down on the line when O.J. is given the ball. Simpson moves but seems to take in the whole situation before committing himself to any one direction. As he strides, he evaluates the picture before him, eleven huge bodies, seven of which are his own men, spaced along the line of scrimmage about 10 yards across from end to end. In a split second, he must decide to cross this line at some point.

"It's like being a jet pilot," O.J. explains. "He's got to think what's three miles ahead of him."

Like the Bionic Man, Simpson employs his magical kinesthetic gift to see through the line and at the barrier beyond. He checks off the possibilities in a flash, some part of his mind calculating the speed of an onrushing linebacker, while at the same instant determining just what it will take to get to a certain point on the field before the secondary rushes up.

Calculus minus the slide rule on a football field.

"I have viable powers," O.J. asserts. "I have very good peripheral vision. I also study the movies and I know where everyone is supposed to be."

Another Simpson secret is revealed: O.J. admits that, unlike other running backs who study opposing linemen, he concentrates only on the linebackers and defensive backs.

"I don't worry about the linemen," he insists. "My men are supposed to clear them out of the way for me. So on the films I watch the other guys for tendencies—if they tackle better with their right shoulder or their left shoulder. If a safety tends to tackle low, say, I pick up my feet. If a linebacker takes a block from my other back, you go outside."

There's usually only one way to meet this sort of genius: pursue O.J. Simpson with a lot of people. Talk to a defensive player and listen to his philosophy: "The main thing with Simpson is to get the first guy to slow him down," he'll say. "Then the other guys have to bring him down. You can't expect one guy to be in position to take him down."

One can only imagine what O.J. becomes when he's allowed to pass the line as a receiver and then is presented with the ball. All havoc results, O.J. darting and dodging in the secondary with only the defensive backs able to pursue.

"Don't try for the big hit on O.J.," says Don Shula, the Miami Dolphins' coach. "O.J.'s got such great moves you'll grab only air. Just try to get a piece of him, then wait for help." Once more, the multiple-tackle theory is proposed for the phantom runner.

When that Jet game was over, O.J. Simpson had broken the record of Jim Brown, the man often compared to him. O.J. had not only broken the legendary Brown's rushing mark, but also for most carries in a season. He surpassed Brown's 305 carries on the same play he surpassed his yardage record. He had gained 200 yards for the second time in succession as well as for the third time in a season, both records. And he had enabled the Buffalo Bills to become the game's first 3,000-yard rushing team.

"I want all the records," O.J. once said, "even though I know they don't mean as much because we play under different circumstances."

When Brown and Simpson are compared, it's usually a tossup, though Larry Brown, the Washington Redskins' former back, said, "O.J. might get the edge because he had to compete against multiple defenses."

Other great runners have offered their analyses. "O.J. senses tacklers," said Gale Sayers, formerly one of football's shiftiest runners. "He makes cuts that are uncanny. It's almost like the guy coming up to the line is yelling, 'Here I come. You better go the other way.' "

Simpson once admitted that he was able to run the way he did because of the extreme cold in Buffalo when he played. Yet despite the temperature hovering around the zero mark, O.J. always wore short-sleeved jerseys, which exposed bare arms.

"I can feel the tacklers better that way," he said. "I can

feel their touch, and in a football game, I just don't want to be touched. The more I feel that way the better the game I play."

Simpson has often insisted that his talents are instinctive. He even claims he is a better runner when he is tired because he thinks less and just reacts. Though his leg strength and balance are tops in the league, he does little to condition them except run. "I don't want to mess with them," he says.

Actually, his legs seem skinny from the knees down. When he was a boy, rickets weakened them. His mother couldn't afford professional care, so he wore his shoes on the wrong feet and used homemade braces. The calcium deficiency left his legs bowed, to which, of course, is what several persons have credited his amazing balance.

Poverty may have been partly responsible for the way his legs looked, but it certainly was responsible for O.J.'s fierce will to break free of ghetto life and into the glamorous world of a professional athlete. Few have been better motivated than O.J. Simpson.

He was the second youngest of four children, all of whom grew up in Potrero Hill, a run-down section of San Francisco. His father left the family when O.J. was four, and his mother raised the children in a project apartment, supporting them on what she made as an orderly at San Francisco General Hospital.

O. J. gravitated toward the gangs that roamed and ruled the area, the Persian Warriors and the Medallions. "I was the leader," he said, "because I was the baddest cat there. You had to be."

But there was one more thing going on in O.J.'s ghetto—sports. At that level, how well you did in sports told you where you stood with your peers. O.J. wanted to be a baseball player.

However, in the middle of his sophomore year in high school, he broke his hand and thus turned to track, where he began to run the sprint races. When he saw how many more girls there were watching track events than there were at baseball games, he gave up baseball for good.

When they found out how fast he could run, they made him go out for football. Because he was big for his age, 160 pounds, he played defensive tackle at first. Then one day it happened; he picked up a fumble and ran for a touchdown. Hollywood stuff. The coach made him a halfback.

Before he was O.J., before that was turned into Orange Juice, and then, simply, the Juice, he was Orenthal, a name his aunt said came from a French actor. When you're a football star and the girls are after you, Orenthal James quickly becomes O.J.

Simpson said Willie Mays was his hero, but not only because of baseball. Willie Mays had a big house, he said, and when O.J. made it in football or any other field, he too was going to have a big house.

Security and fame have gone hand in hand with Simpson, who has never denied such reasons for his success. His wife called him "a homebody who wants a roof over his head first of all and three meals a day." That's what is really important in the long run.

Even today, O.J. Simpson wears the smartest clothes, drives the flashiest cars and visits the classiest spots because of such early conditioning. He even carries a box of John Player cigarettes, not to smoke, which he doesn't, but because he likes the snappy box they come in. He wore white shoes in the game in which he ran for 250 yards, and he kept on wearing them afterward.

"Look at me," he likes to say. "I ain't just like everybody else on this field."

This is how O.J. explains it: "I never had anything. I never owned anything. We lived in the poor section of town. We were always paying off on our furniture. Suddenly, when you realize you can buy yourself and your family anything you want, you go out and do it."

O.J. says he stole when he was a kid. He knew the feeling he had when he had money in his pocket. But it also made him understand how to talk to and help kids today who are in the same situation as he was. "I want to be a social worker when I finish in sports," he says. "I want to show them what a kid from their side of town can amount to if he puts his mind to it."

O.J. chose Southern California for the following reason: He saw a man in a white horse gallop on the field during halftime of a football game, and it so impressed him he announced right then that U.S.C. was where he was going.

The college can thank him. When his amazing career there had ended, he had played in 21 games and carried 674 times for 3,423 yards, an average of more than 5 yards a rush. He had scored 36 touchdowns, broken the college records for carries, yards gained, and a dozen others. While he played, U.S.C. won 18 games, lost 2, and tied 1.

The winner of the Heisman Trophy as the greatest football player in the country, O.J. was being hailed as the greatest college runner of all time. With a four-year $250,000 contract with the Bills, plus endorsements and publishing deals that figured to raise his short-term income to almost $1 million, he was also the richest rookie to enter the pro game.

But he found the first three seasons in the league the toughest and most discouraging he had ever faced. The strength that O.J. Simpson proved to have inside him kept him going until he was able to achieve his goals.

"The trip of being a football player," he said, "is that when you're hot, you're really hot. When you're on top, everybody wants to be with you, the kids look up to you and listen to you, everything is fun. It was always that way for me at U.S.C. Maybe it was too easy. When I wasn't on top anymore in Buffalo, I didn't feel like I was all the way down, but I did waste too much time blaming the coach or bad luck. Now I can look back and see that some of the things that were happening were my own fault. I had to do some changing of my own. In a way, I had to grow up again."

O.J. credits Lou Saban, his coach at Buffalo, for saving his career. Not only did Saban start by surrounding the young and talented runner with first-rate blockers, he helped alter his attitude. Soon O.J. was extolling his team, his blockers, his coach, and everything about the game. Soon O.J. was the Juice and running loose in the N.F.L.

"Football is basically a numbers game at the point of attack," O.J. has said. "The ideal situation is to get four men blocking only three tacklers. But if we at least clear enough of their guys out to leave me one-on-one with the last tackler, that's cool, because one-on-one is my game."

Then Simpson adds another startling fact: "I've often said that all great runners have to be insane. I mean, they can't be acting out of logic or thought. They get into a certain rhythm and make instinctive moves without any reason for them.

"Somebody told me that he once asked Pancho Gonzales what foot he hit his backhand off, and Pancho had to think about it before he answered. It's that way with a back. I can't always tell you what I did to get into the end zone."

Insane runners are the ones who get injured the fastest, right? Wrong, at least with O.J. Simpson, that is. Yet, he sees it as no mere coincidence. "I don't go looking to stick my head in where it can get broken," he says.

O.J. remembers the first time he faced Dick Butkus, probably the toughest and fiercest tackler of all the linebackers who have played the game. "Some guys said to me you had to challenge Butkus and show him you can hit with him," O.J. said.

"I said, 'Hell, no, I want to show him that I'm so quick, he can't hit me.'

"That's the way I feel. If I'm doing my job, nobody should get a clear shot to hit me and hurt me. I admire

Larry Brown for his courage in hitting tacklers head-on, but beat up is what it got him. He didn't do himself any favors. I wanted to stay in one piece so I could be part of a championship."

Not only a championship, but immortality. Simpson became the first athlete since Babe Ruth to have a stadium built for him when the Buffalo Bills constructed the 80,020-seat Rich Stadium.

Besides O.J.'s E.S.P., the most breathtaking facet of his ability was that the more he carried the ball in a game, the better he got. He could not be intimidated. In the face of fatigue, he was indefatigable. An entire defense was more likely to wane and lose its concentration before Simpson did.

One rival coach referred to O.J. as the sooner-or-later back. "Sooner or later," he said, "no matter how hard you make it for him, O.J. will beat you. Eight, ten, or twenty carries, no matter how many times he gets stacked up, no matter how much muscle you lay on him, he does not discourage. Let up on the twenty-first play and he's in the end zone. He has brought back to pro football that forgotten dimension—the great running back who actually gets tougher the more tired he seems to be."

Simpson can explain this quality. He claims that at the start of a game an offensive player's mind is a hive of scouting reports and his own apprehensions. He is thinking as much as he is acting and therefore becomes tentative.

"That's why you'll see me go off by myself, away from the conversation. I tell guys, 'Get away from me with all that stuff,' because it ruins your head. Eventually, I reach a point where I stop trying to outthink the defense and begin to react instinctively to the situation—to what a guy does, whether he's trying to handle me one-on-one, whether he can take a shoulder or a head feint. I know instinctively what to expect. The more tired I get, the better I react. It's like a fighter who's hurt and fights better because he's fighting instinctively."

Because he is so elusive, the opposition has shown a reluctance to hit him too hard on the first pop. They might miss. So that fact has preserved his health. That and his bow-leggedness, which distributes his weight as if over an arch, help lessen the impact of tackles.

"Yes, he's less prone to injury," says his coach. "Most knee injuries occur from a lateral hit combined with rotation. A man gets hit from the side and his knee turns. But Simpson's bowleggedness prevents this."

O.J. has never studied films of his style. He doesn't really know what he does, other than that he does it. So the invariable comparisons to Gale Sayers and Jim Brown crop up from time to time.

Sayers was a 6-foot, 198-pound back for the Chicago Bears who probably got to the line of scrimmage faster than any other name runner. He was a slasher who moved downfield with power, speed, and quickness, and he held the old record of 22 touchdowns. But he didn't have the same ability to "run to daylight" that Simpson showed. If a hole was closed to Sayers, he didn't veer to find another hole as well as O.J. did.

Before Simpson arrived, the rushing-yardage record for a season belonged to Jimmy Brown of the Cleveland Browns. He was one of the first backs for whom "option blocking" actually worked well—you take out a man on the line any way you can and hope your runner will run the right way. Brown had balance and power, but at 6 feet 2 and 228 pounds, he did not have Simpson's speed.

"I can run over a lot of people," O.J. has said. "But I only do that if I have to. I can outrun most people, too, and I keep that in reserve when I need it. Sometimes when I know I can't get away, I'll just run straight at my tackler. After I've smashed into him, I'll look for his number. Then later in the game, if I can, I'll run at him again.

"Often I would see the guy tighten up, become flat-footed and tense, waiting for me to make that first move. That's when I would have him," O.J. said, laughing softly.

"Sometimes I run broken-field, like Sayers. Some years I want to run with power, like Brown. It's hard to do both. It's all in the mind. When you see a guy coming at you, you want to bowl him over, but at the same time you see some daylight and you change strategy.

"Often I start out to be a Jim Brown and switch to Gale Sayers in the middle of a run. How many guys can be both?"

There is only one answer: O.J. Simpson.

# 2

# MUHAMMAD ALI

## A Mind as Quick as His Body

Of all the names in this book, one is easily the most recognizable throughout the world. Say "Muhammad Ali" in New York or Sri Lanka, in Moscow or Mali, in Nome or Tahiti, and faces will light up even if you cannot speak a word of that country's language. On the wings of his mercurial feet, the heavyweight power of his fists, the joyful spirit of his soul and the incredible record of his boxing heroics, Muhammad Ali has become the most famous man in the world.

Of his universal popularity, there can be no argument. On the basis of his mastery of a primeval sport like prizefighting, he may very well be the most astonishing athlete of our time. Besides living his own legend and winning the world heavyweight championship three separate times—no one else ever did that—his talents far outgrew the confines of sport, overflowing into religion, politics, philosophy, race, theater, literature, and life itself. Muhammad Ali virtually evolved into a cult.

All because, you might say, he was able to best every challenger to his throne inside the "squared circle," where, as Joe Louis once said, "You can run but you can't hide." The fight game was Ali's vehicle, and to succeed, it still came down to one man against another—Ali vs. anybody— who wanted to be where Ali was.

Another amazing aspect of his story is that Ali did not triumph in every one of these duels. He actually was proved quite mortal. He possessed faults, did some things to excess, made mistakes, and even looked foolish at times. Yet, Ali always came away unmarked, inside the ring as well as outside it, and he came back to win and retire as the champion.

One of the keys to Ali's success has been his ability to innovate. In fact, there never has been a fighter who could improvise so brilliantly at the same moment that such cunning was called for. This is not the same thing as preparing for a bout, game strategy, or any sort of special event. When something extraordinary seemed necessary for him

**17**

to stave off defeat or might make winning more spectacular than it would have been, Ali rose to new heights of improvisation.

Take the "Ali Shuffle," a simple enough maneuver that a dancer might create for effect. In the middle of a fight, though, such a crazy-like war dance caused fight experts to debate its value as well as to praise it. Some persons even called Ali a showoff or a braggart because of the shuffle, but it made news.

What many people forget is that the Ali Shuffle became a psychological symbol as well as a strategic ploy. It told an opponent that he was not only looking at the world's fastest, cleverest, and most confident human, but that he was also up against a superfighter who had so much speed tucked away in his body he could never tire.

The shuffle, though just a dance, could destroy an opponent's concentration, too, as some men tried desperately to make up for being made fun of. That was when Ali had his man where he wanted him. Ali's best weapons, whether in words or flamboyancy, were psychological.

Remember the "rope-a-dope"? No one had heard of this term for leaning back against the ropes while protecting your face with your gloves and your body with your arms and ducking and dodging as a heavy-handed fighter pounded you with the hardest blows he could throw. As history proved, Ali wore out the best and strongest hitters of his day with just such a strategy. What's more, he thought of it on the spur of the moment.

Of course, not everybody could get away with such a plan. Ali, because of his great speed, superior judgment of where punches were going to land, plus a tall frame that allowed him to bend far back and out of reach, became the perfect instigator of the rope-a-dope. Once his opponent had exhausted himself, Ali turned to the attack and found it a cinch to knock out his weary adversary.

"Float like a butterfly, sting like a bee" became Ali's theme. But it was a lot more than a pretty phrase; it was true. Ali, with the ballet dancer's legs, could move about the ring like a sylph. He was far faster than most of his heavyweight rivals, and even if they did prove equal in quickness, they certainly couldn't match his physical size.

Ali's body was deceptive. It was so well proportioned that many a fighter entering the ring to take him on was taken aback by the size of him. It made a superb fighting machine—those wide shoulders tapering down to smooth thighs and midsection. Yet, it disguised the thickness of his chest and the muscles of his legs, making him seem smaller and slighter until . . . you met him face-on.

When the "butterfly" factor became neutralized, Ali could then assume the weapons of the "bee," meaning a stiff jab, a blindingly fast right-hand uppercut or a straight punch delivered with all the force of his body. Speed *and* punch. When you had the best of both these attributes like Ali, there was not much you could do to escape being successful.

Was Ali considered a powerful puncher? Not really, which is another paradox. In his first twenty fights—when he was known as Cassius Clay, his given name—he won 17 of them by knockout. His average of knockouts per number of fights was well over .750, one of the best ever. How could a so-called nonslugger accomplish this?

The answer lay in speed and timing. Along with his skill at throwing punches so extremely fast, he also picked the perfect moment to let them go—in other words, just before his opponent was able to anticipate it. It's called "not seeing the punch." It doesn't matter how hard the punch was, but rather that the receiver didn't expect it. That's what recorded knockouts for Ali.

"He jabs you sweet and cool," was the way Willie Pastrano, a former light-heavyweight champion, described Ali's stinging left. Films showed that Ali's jabs were one-third faster than those of Sugar Ray Robinson, the brilliant middleweight often considered the world's best fighter pound for pound. Add such quickness to a body suitable for playing football, and you come up with the awesome combination of an Ali.

Being as fast as lightning is not only confusing to an opponent, but it also can cover up for whatever faults one has. Eddie Futch, a well-known trainer, was one who claimed that Ali had so much natural ability he never had to learn all the fundamentals. Ali could outrun any mistake.

"Defense ain't the hands as much as the legs," Ali says. So by dancing, using his speed, and exercising his superb judgment, Ali could escape danger by what looked like a whisker. Sometimes he even let his hands drop, stuck his face out to invite a punch, and then snapped it back. Imagine the frustration this created in his opponent.

Because he could think and move so much faster than his foe, Ali had the time to accomplish such a psych job, for psychology was what it was all about. Once you have an opponent thinking, it brings on real concern, and when that occurs the battle is half over. Of course, it's easier to explain this than accomplish it. That is what made Ali so extraordinary against fighters who were "too smart and too clever" to be psyched—but were, anyway.

Ali developed this psyching-out to an art. He seemed to be born with the ability to transform certain feelings of ineptness to whomever he fought. By pulling away from a punch, by carrying his hands ridiculously low, by punching only to his opponents' heads, Ali would be working this special kind of magic. The result: It made them think they were tired. Once you think you are tired, you are tired. Ali always hit his opponents a lot more than they hit him. Once again, frustration.

No one knew what Ali would do, though, when he entered a ring. Not his manager, trainer, closest friends, or family. He was astonishingly unpredictable. You never knew if he'd come into a fight fat or lean. You never knew if he would box or slug it out. The only thing you knew was that you were in for a surprise. Unfortunately for his opponents, they didn't know, either, and they were the ones most affected.

If he hadn't been Muhammad Ali, the world's most famous man, he might not have been allowed to perform such antics in a prizefight. Sometimes it proved degrading, not only to him and his opponent, but to the fight game in general.

In his first year as a pro, he fought a fighter named Ron Draper. In the last round, he took a light tap on the head from Draper. Ali began his act, pretending to be seriously hurt, swaying and wobbling and then falling in a heap on the canvas. He got up at the count of nine and continued acting like a fighter in the last stages of being knocked out, reeling around the ring, teetering and showing the whites of his eyes. Hc would back into the ropes and then come bouncing off them so fast he was jettisoned to the other side. As he bounced back and forth like a drunk on a yo-yo, Draper would try to hit him. But Ali would pirouette out of reach and stumble to the floor. It was a crass bit of showmanship in a fight Ali had won easily in the earlier rounds. It did him no honor. But it did cause talk.

Next to fighting, talking has been Ali's greatest strength. His skill at speaking on almost any subject and doing so extemporaneously fascinated his public. It gave him tremendous charisma, too, as well as inviting criticism. Some people considered him a pop-off.

"I'll never understand that," said Angelo Dundee, his manager. "When I was growing up, Joe Louis was acclaimed as a great fighter and looked down on because he didn't say much. Now we have Ali who both talks and fights, and there's resentment."

Besides being considered a "loudmouth," a "lousy" oral poet, and a "second-rate comedian," Ali was credited for being vocally honest. He said what was on his mind, which can be a lot better than becoming a hypocrite.

21

One columnist described Ali this way: "Part Demosthenes, part Billy Graham, part Edgar Guest, and part Flip Wilson, hardly the best of each, but surely the loudest." All of them added up to Ali, the consummate actor who used the ring as his stage to tell the world off.

You may be asking: Is Ali really a smart guy? The answer depends on what you mean by "smart." He is not a good reader, writes hesitatingly, and is helpless with numbers or statistics. He cannot reason in a rational manner, nor can he think through most of the subjects he mouths off on.

What Ali has, however, is instinct. Some have called it "street sense." He limits his factual knowledge to what most concerns his life: boxing, morality, publicity, travel. Because he has charisma, he can charm a critic, a group—even a nation. But Ali is never deep.

Ali also has a classic case of "ego." His boxing skills and consummate acting ability could carry this off, however. One of his most celebrated gimmicks, his prediction of what round he would knock out his opponent, in rhyme yet, stemmed from his refusal to hold back this cockiness. Actually, it was a game at first and exceeded even Ali's wildest dreams, and thus became part of the whole picture.

It probably began in 1962, just after Ali had won the Olympic light-heavyweight gold medal. In his first fight in Madison Square Garden, Ali took advantage of New York's publicity and said half in jest: "The man must fall in the round I call." He was fighting a man named Sonny Banks. When reporters asked him what round, Ali said, "Banks must fall in four." When he did, everyone was amazed, Ali probably most of all. Yet, he said: "See, I told you so." And thus another legend was under way.

Sometimes, his predictions got Ali into trouble. When he fought Henry Cooper, the English champion, in 1963, Ali said: "I hand you no jive, Coop falls in five." After two rounds, Cooper, a notorious bleeder, could hardly see out of a cut eye, but Ali decided to coast until the fifth round.

In the fourth, Cooper connected with a wild left hook that floored Ali, only the second time in his career he had been knocked down. He wobbled back to the corner, at the bell, but in the fifth, he did knock Cooper out.

In one of his most important fights, Ali's prediction not only backfired but he lost the fight as well, when Joe Frazier defeated him in fifteen rounds in 1971. Before that bout with Frazier, who was undefeated and had won the championship while Ali was under suspension for refusing to be drafted, Ali, also still undefeated, was asked to predict the outcome. He said: "Joe's got two chances, slim and none." That wisecrack was replayed many times in Ali's presence to try and deflate his ego. It seldom succeeded.

Another one of Ali's stages was the prefight ceremony, or weighing in. It never really meant anything since heavyweights can come in at any weight, so its purposes have usually been for extra publicity. Until Ali came along, no one understood what prefight publicity was.

When Ali changed all that, it drew hundreds of reporters, broadcasters, hangers-on, and TV cameras. Ali was now in his element; his opponent out of his. So Ali took advantage of it, not only ranting and raving, which made news (and entertainment), but also helping to unnerve his future opponent.

Ali's antics caused pandemonium and hit the nerve center of his bewildered opponents. They would lose control of their emotions, grow terribly angry, lose their "cool," and be reduced to childishness.

Some called Ali a ham. Others said his need to act outlandish was a ploy to fend off the fear he felt inside. The truth was neither of these or both. Once Ali got his act in gear, it was as if he couldn't stop it. Then, when he realized the value of the script, he had no intention of stopping it. It was a sure way to keep from getting bored.

According to a Madison Square Garden official, Ali acted no differently when he was Clay. "He was the same then as he is now," said the official. "He cried for attention.

He used to stand on the corner outside the Garden just to see how many people would recognize him."

A quick look at Clay's early years might provide the clues leading to such a strong desire to be known. When he was a little boy in school, he was known to be different. He found out early, he says, that to be noticed, you had to be eccentric. So instead of taking the school bus like all the other children, Cassius ran to school alongside it, with all the kids yelling and waving at him. From the time he can remember, Ali says, he felt like somebody special.

At the age of twelve, he entered the gym and took up fighting. He showed such aptitude that he was pampered like a spoiled brat. "I've not worked at a real job in my whole life," he admits. Luckily, his mother and father were a model couple and provided young Cassius with love and security.

Joe Martin was Clay's early instructor in the art of boxing. Martin said that Clay was a troublemaker from the outset, that he was loud and brash and made so much noise that he had to kick him out of the gym. And he was not very popular either because he bragged even then. "He said he was better than anybody at fighting and that he'd be the champion someday," said Martin.

Later, Clay became Ali and discovered there was humor to be made out of bragging. After that came the poetic utterances, also good for a laugh and a story or two. Following that, Ali took a stand and denounced the Vietnam war, which brought the wrath of the government down on his head and stripped him of the heavyweight championship. Finally, Ali entered the racial struggle and avowed his conversion to Islam. That's why he changed his name in the Muslim fashion of the day.

Early on, Ali had learned what the benefits might be from taking the villain's or "wrong" side of an issue. He explained it this way:

"When I began fighting seriously, I saw that grown-up people acted like the school kids of my youth, especially the

24

fight fans. Almost from my first fight, I'd mouth off to anybody how I was going to do to whoever I was going to fight.
People would go out of their way to come and see, hoping,
of course, that I'd get beat.

"When I was no more than a preliminary fighter, they'd
put me on a card because I was a drawing card. I was a
draw because I talked a lot. The minute I'd appear, the fans
would yell, 'Kill 'im!' or 'Bash in his nose!' I didn't care what
they said as long as they kept coming to see me."

Two years after Ali had won the championship from
Sonny Liston, he was classified 1-A in the draft. It was
when reporters asked him how he felt about it that he
made the famed remark: "I ain't got no quarrels with them
Viet Congs."

When he claimed to be a conscientious objector, he
was suspended from boxing by the Boxing Commission.
That order also took away his crown, and he drifted in exile
for three years. By then, public feeling toward the war had
turned the other way, in Ali's favor, and finally he was allowed to resume fighting.

His fight against Joe Frazier, the champion, has been
called The Fight, meaning one of the best fights of all time
and certainly one of Ali's best if not The Best. Both men
fought all-out for fifteen rounds. Frazier, a nonstop puncher
and body-punisher with a wicked hook to the head, against
the clever danseur Ali, who stung you over and over with
his brutal jab and flicking right hand.

Ali tried his speed-and-run. He went into his rope-a-
dope (before it even had an official name) and he even tried
to slug it out. But Frazier's hook caught him in the four-
teenth and Ali lost the decision, which was very close.

Neither fighter was much good after that fight. Though
Ali lost, he did manage to recover better than Frazier, who
seemed never to regain his complete skills. They met two
more times, with Ali winning both.

His most amazing battle, if not his artistic best, was
his championship epic against Foreman in Zaire, Africa, in

1974. Foreman was the champion, having destroyed Frazier to get it. Foreman was a heavy favorite to beat and destroy Ali as well. But this was where the rope-a-dope became the No. 1 topic of the day as Ali took Foreman's hardest punches and then knocked out his exhausted foe in the eighth.

Foreman may have given himself (and his lack of stamina) away before the fight when he said, trying to outbrag Ali: "I don't like fights. I just land the right punch and everything is over. Nobody gets hurt and nobody gets killed." Ali took advantage of Foreman's inexperience at long fights.

So now Ali was champion for the second time, tying the record held by Floyd Patterson. But Ali was to lose the title once more to a young man named Leon Spinks and then beat Spinks in a return match that gave him the championship for a third and record time. Ali retired with the crown intact, but made an abortive effort to win it a fourth time from Larry Holmes.

Just before he made that fateful decision, Ali's manager, Angelo Dundee, said of him: "You know, he's still a nice kid. The easiest fighter I ever had. He was really unspoiled from the beginning. He changed around the whole charisma of boxing, but he remained the nice kid I used to give a deuce to stay loose."

The reason: "Because Ali *likes* boxing," Dundee added. "That's the key to Ali. He *likes* the sport."

Dundee went on to explain how the best times for Ali and him were early in the morning, after a 5 A.M. run and workout, when nobody was up and just the two of them would sit around and talk boxing.

"Ali survived every kind of situation," Dundee continued, "because he wanted to be a fighter. He used to walk from the hotel to the gym, which was about five miles away."

To be great, one must be dedicated, and according to Dundee, Ali wanted to box every day and with everybody.

Every day he would come to the gym and ask Dundee to give him someone to fight.

"His happiest moments were there in the gym," Dundee noted. "He'd get energized. Other fighters aren't like that. The gym is a problem to them. They hate to go; they hate to work. So, this was the thing that made Ali so great.

"He loved what he did."

# 3

# ROD CAREW

## Unique in His Own Way

ROD CAREW

One of baseball's fondest truisms used to be: "Singles hitters drive Fords, but home-run hitters drive Cadillacs." Two things changed that kind of thinking: the energy crisis and Rod Carew.

When you win the batting championship of your league seven times, as Carew did, you not only can drive whatever car you want, you also get paid handsomely and you get mentioned in the same company as Ty Cobb and Ted Williams, two of baseball's all-time greatest hitters. Yet, all this happened despite the fact Carew never hit more than 14 home runs in one season.

Carew began making Cobb worshipers sit up and compare when he won his first American League batting title in 1969 with a .332 average and then reeled off four more titles between 1972 and 1975 (.318, .350, .364, and .359). It would have been seven in a row except for the fact that Carew lost the 1976 championship by .002 of a point before going on to be top dog again in 1977 (.388) and '78 (.333). Only Cobb with 12 titles and Honus Wagner with eight have captured more batting championships. Carew, of course, is still going strong.

Rod made Williams idolizers take notice when he threatened the sacred .400 mark during several seasons. Williams was the last batter to reach that mark when he hit .406 in 1941.

But Carew has constantly flirted with the .400 mark, finishing with .388 in '77, the highest average in the majors in twenty years. Carew missed seven games that year but still wound up with 239 hits and 100 runs batted in. If he had had eight more hits, he would have batted .400.

"Rod Carew doesn't have to hit .400," asserted his manager at Minnesota, Gene Mauch. "He doesn't have to prove anything. All he has to do is retire and wait for the Hall of Fame to call."

Carew doesn't have to hit home runs, either. In 1972, Carew won the batting title without hitting a homer. In eighty years of baseball, only two other batting champions

31

(Ginger Beaumont in 1902 and Zack Wheat in 1918) went homerless.

His lifetime batting average of .334 separates Carew from his nearest active rival by 22 points. And the year he hit .388, the next highest average was Dave Parker's .338, making the fifty-point spread the widest in modern baseball history.

Besides being able to produce hits, Carew is a superb baserunner and fielder. He has stolen home sixteen times, high among active players. In 1969 he stole home seven times, breaking Cobb's league record and tying Pete Reiser's major-league mark. As a first baseman, he missed winning the Golden Glove for best fielder by a single percentage point.

What all of Rod Carew's magnificent feats add up to is this: He undertook one of the most difficult tasks in sport and conquered it, absolutely and brilliantly. He took a bat that measures less than three inches in diameter at its widest point and tried to hit a baseball, also not quite three inches in diameter. The cylindrical object meeting head-on with a spherical object.

The job is not an easy one, as thousands of major-leaguers know. First of all, there's the terrific speed at which a pitcher throws the ball, well over ninety miles an hour, which can travel the 60 feet 6 inches from mound to plate in 2/5 of a second. All one has to do if he's a batter is connect well enough to hit the ball safely and reach base just three out of ten times to become a celebrated .300 batter.

Hit even slightly better than three out of ten and your name is sought on bubble-gum cards, at banquets, for endorsements, and on long-term lucrative contracts with any team you want to play for. So here's a guy named Carew who can accomplish the task closer to four out of ten. No wonder he's acclaimed as baseball's premier batsman.

Let's examine Carew's physical attributes. He's 6 feet tall, weighs 182 pounds, and has the wrists and forearms of a heavyweight boxer (he's always lifted weights).

Here's one secret: His face is thin and angular, so with a chunk of chewing tobacco bulging out his cheek, Carew looks like an old-timer who's returned to haunt the modern ballparks.

"But it gives me a better view of the pitch," explains Carew cryptically. "When the chaw is tucked in there, it makes my skin tight. When the skin is tight like that, you can't squinch your eye, which means more of your eye is on the ball. It's important not to squinch up at the plate."

So much for Carew's "chewing tobacco" secret of hitting. However, there's a lot more to major-league batting than that, or else tobacco companies would be besieged by .200 hitters.

Actually, Carew possesses about the sharpest eyes in baseball. He says he can spot the ball—its speed and rotation—as soon as it leaves the pitcher's fingertips. "I can tell by the rotation if it's a curve, slider, or fastball," he says. He also insists he can see his bat strike the ball.

Amos Otis of the Kansas City Royals said: "Trying to sneak a fastball past Rod is like trying to sneak the sunrise past a rooster."

Trim and muscular, Carew bats left while throwing right-handed. He seems to have a different stance for every pitcher he meets, but he claims he's broken it down to just twelve basic positions. "You want to baffle the pitcher mainly," he says, "and you want to get yourself comfortable."

In the batter's box, Carew stands as deep as he can, which gives him even another split-second to size up the pitch. "Most batters like to guess what's coming," he points out, "but not me. I just wait to see what the pitch is and then I swing."

Carew can be so smooth and effortless at the plate that he looks lackadaisical. Some players think he's not trying as hard as he should be, but the reason is that Carew has so much raw talent he doesn't have to fuss and look agitated at the plate.

Williams, an ultraconnoisseur of batsmanship, once pointed out that besides Carew's good forearms and well-molded body, he had long, strong fingers and big veins. The long fingers give him his amazing bat control, while the superveins provide perfect circulation.

The bat Carew uses is top-heavy, 34½ inches long with a skinny handle and a bottle end. That kind requires powerful arms and hands to maneuver. Said one teammate: "Carew handles a bat like a pickup stick."

Carew can make adjustments whenever he is bothered by certain pitches. When pitchers begin feeding him inside stuff because he seemed to be troubled by them, he quickly developed a wrist movement allowing him to slap the ball to left field. When pitchers tried soft stuff or changeups on him, Carew merely changed his stance and began powdering slow pitches.

"He has fantastic eye-hand coordination," Mauch said of Carew. "You have to in order to hit the ball so hard so often."

Even a spitball pitcher (anonymous) found his wet deliveries could not fool Carew. "That's all I throw him, and he still hits them," said the pitcher. "He's the only player in baseball who consistently hits my grease. He sees the ball so well, I guess he can pick out the dry side."

Carew will hold his bat low to give him a quicker swing through the ball. Against left-handed pitchers, he uses an open stance. Against righthanders, he closes his legs and keeps them more parallel to the plate. When he comes up against a fastballer like Nolan Ryan, (now in the National League), he will spread his legs a little wider and put more weight on his back foot.

"When you step up to the plate," Carew says, "your total concentration has to be on one place, the pitcher's mound. A lot of guys see a hole and will try to hit it there. But you can't until you pick the pitch up."

Carew considers himself a free-swinger and claims he doesn't try to guide the ball through holes. He also avoids the common pitfall of modern batters: trying to pull a pitch over the wall. Carew long ago eliminated the lust for the long ball, one of the major reasons he has kept his average so high. Trying to cream a pitcher's best pitch is the fastest way to strike out, Carew will tell you.

Carew's hits include line drives, slashing pokes through the infield, bunts, Baltimore chops, Texas-leaguers, and topped balls he beats out. Every part of the ballpark is Carew territory. He can pull, slice, or go with the pitch. Pitchers hate him, naturally. For, unlike with Williams, there is no shift a team can employ to stop Carew's 90-degree spray of base hits.

Now we've come to the crux of the matter. Carew is a student of his own ability. It's as if he's given himself an aptitude test and from that, he's determined what it is he can do best as a baseball player. Disdaining the long ball, except when necessary, he has become the thinking man's hitter, always studying the pitchers, observing the fielders and going for the percentages. Like a gambler, he has searched for the "sure thing," but unlike a gambler, he has found it.

The answer lies within himself: Don't get greedy; take what you can get, and don't overextend the limits of your talent. Carew's finest attribute was in teaching himself what most batters never learn: That there is more room inside a ball park's fences for a ball to land than in the stands.

"He's got control of his whole game," said Bill Freehan, the former Detroit Tiger catcher. "He never lets it get away."

"There's no way you can play him," said Bill North when he was with Oakland, "because he can hit with enough power to keep you back deep so you can't play him like he's going to drop everything right over the infield. And he can drop it over the infield. Rod Carew is in a class all by himself."

Carew has tried to explain himself, saying: "What a lot of people don't realize is that certain guys on certain clubs have a job to do. My job is to get on base, to try and hit the ball somewhere. On Minnesota (where Harmon Killebrew, a leading home-run hitter, and Tony Oliva, a leader in r.b.i.'s played), we had guys who could drive in runs. But they had to have somebody on base to do it.

"Every hitter knows his capabilities. I know mine. Oh, I could hit the ball hard if I wanted to. But if I hit 10 home runs, I'm not going to help the club. If I get on base and score 95 runs, I am."

Carew admits his favorite kind of hit is one "just one inch or two outside a guy's reach. Maybe he cheated over a step in the other direction on me, and I kept him honest."

But then Carew insists he doesn't try to place the ball through holes, just sprays it around. When he hits the ball constantly to the opposite field, say, he'll notice that they'll start moving everybody over to the left side against him. So what happens? Bam, down the first-base line it will go.

This takes a lot of practice, which a lot of major-leaguers can't be bothered with. Carew can. "I've disciplined myself to know what I can do with the bat. I know who I am and I know who I'm not. It's not a shame to go to the opposite field. It's not a shame to lay a bunt down."

A major reason Carew hits for so high an average is that he rarely suffers a slump as most batters do from time to time. His speed in legging out infield hits helps prevent a possible slump, but the most sure-fire method is bunting.

They say Carew can lay down a bunt better than anyone since Phil Rizzuto. Once in spring training he challenged a teammate to toss a sweater onto the infield, then rolled a bunt into its enveloping folds. The sweater was moved; he bunted dead center again. More than a dozen times, first on the third-base line, then the first-base side, he put the ball exactly on target.

"Bunting gives me 25 points a year on my batting average," Carew explains. "But you've got to learn how to bunt in each ballpark. The ball rolls differently in every park.

"One year I bunted 27 times and got 20 hits. Seven of those hits came with two strikes. Bat control!"

Watching Carew in batting practice gives a perfect indication of bat control. First, he bunts. One backspins to a dead halt about 1½ feet inside the line and fifteen feet toward third base. The next bunt curls to a stop near the line halfway toward first. Then Carew strokes a ball off the left-field wall on one hop, hits a shot back at the pitcher that caroms off the protective wire screen, and, finally, sends a line drive over the first-base bag. He finishes up with two hit-and-run grounders that skid just beyond the lunges of the shortstop and the second baseman.

Managers will tell you that Carew sneaks up on a team. He dribbles one here, bunts one there, drills one through the middle, and so on. You don't realize until you look at the box score the next day that Carew had three hits.

"Even when they know I'm going to bunt, they can't throw me out," says Carew with disarming confidence. "I see the third baseman advancing in while I'm up, but I can drop the ball to a spot where he will have an awkward throw. He will have to come up clean with the ball and throw on the run. Not too many third basemen can do that consistently."

Blessed with excellent speed, Carew's ability to place the ball where he wants to makes him almost unique. Says Carl Yastrzemski of the Boston Red Sox: "I've never seen Carew go into a bad streak, and it's on account of his speed. If he hits a ball to either side of a fielder, he can probably beat it out."

Yastrzemski was asked if other players could add points to their average by not overswinging. "No," said Yaz, "Rod's just an exception. I think if he wanted to, he could turn around and hit 25 or 30 home runs and sacrifice his average a little. He's got pretty good power. But he'd rather hurt you by getting base hits and stealing second, third, and home."

When Carew stole home a record seven times, his manager was Billy Martin (who is also the godfather of

Carew's older daughter, Charryse). "I taught him how to steal home," Martin says. "That's all I ever taught him. He's always known how to hit."

Carew's way of moving looks effortless and sometimes lulls pitchers and fielders into forgetting how fast he is. "I still go from first to third faster than most guys," Carew says.

Besides his legs, Carew covets his bats and often credits them with his success. He can tell by just lifting one if his bat is minutely out of order. He once sent a shipment of bats back to Hillerich & Bradsby, maker of the Louisville Slugger, explaining: "Every one was the wrong weight, and the handles were all too big." No one else could tell, but the wood had not been shaved to within the proper tiny fraction of an inch.

Carew cares for his bats as if they were babies. He bathes them with alcohol, removing the buildup of pine tar that is used to tighten the bond between hand and wood. "I can't stand a dirty bat," he says. "Some guys leave pine tar on their bats and never clean them. I can't understand that. How can they get a feel for the wood?"

His bats are so valuable to him that he locks them in a closet in the clubhouse near the sauna. "The heat of the sauna bakes out the bad wood," Carew explains.

In the dugout, Carew keeps his bats away from the team's collection, which anybody can grab. "I see guys bang their bats against the dugout steps after they make an out," he says. "That bruises them and makes them weaker. I couldn't do that. I baby my bats, treat them like my kids, because using a bat is how I make my living."

According to his wife, Marilynn, Carew is like any superachiever. "He has more drive buried deep inside him than an average person. And I think he'll tell you that baseball, especially the hitting, has always been an outlet, maybe even an escape of sorts."

Carew had an unusual early life. He was born on a train while his mother was traveling from her home in Panama to the doctor. He was named after Dr. Rodney Cline, the physician who happened to be on the train and delivered him.

"We were poor, really poor," Carew says. "I almost never had shoes or clothes good enough to go to church and Sunday school like the other kids. But no matter what, my mother always saw that I had baseball shoes and a glove. She knew how much the game meant to me."

Carew developed his quick wrists and fast swing in pickup games in Panama. He grew up playing with rag balls wound in tape, while his prized possession was a Ted Williams bat he had won for his superior play in Little League. His dream at that time was always the same: Go to the United States and become a big-league baseball player.

When he was fifteen, his mother immigrated to New York City and, after finding a home and a job, sent for Rod, his brother, and three sisters. His high school (George Washington in Manhattan) didn't have a baseball team, so Carew played in a sandlot league, where he was discovered by a Minnesota scout not far from Yankee Stadium.

At that time, he was a 6-footer with a skinny body that made no one think of a home-run slugger. But when he stepped into the batting cage under the scrutiny of the scout, he started blasting the ball. In fact, he hit so many balls over the fence that the scout ordered him out of the cage, yelling: "Get him out of here before somebody sees the kid!" A month later, Rod Carew signed with the Minnesota Twins for a $5,000 bonus.

He was named the American League's rookie of the year, and in 1977 the Baseball Writers Association of America voted him the league's most valuable player. Carew's response was: "All this publicity has been great for me, but it's not going to make me different. I'll always look back to what I had as a kid. I know where I came from."

One thing Carew is prouder of than baseball awards, he says, is the Medal of Honor given to him by Panama. "I'm the only athlete ever to have won it," he said proudly. Although he has lived in the U.S. longer than in Panama, he has not sought American citizenship. He explains:

"I've kept my citizenship because to most kids down there, I'm a national hero, someone they look up to. I think if I became a U.S. citizen they would think that I let them down."

It doesn't seem to matter what country he represents when he is at the plate with a bat in his hands. His opponents just about concede him two hits a game. If they worry about trying to hold him to anything under that, they could wind up as frustrated as a third baseman named Ken McMullen once did.

As the third baseman for the California Angels, McMullen held a reputation as one of the slickest fielders in the game. When Carew batted for the first time against California, McMullen moved in looking for the bunt. Carew laid down a beauty and beat the throw to first.

The second time Carew came up, McMullen moved in a bit closer than before, and still Carew's bunt allowed him to beat the throw to first. On his third at-bat, Carew saw McMullen advance as close to the plate as he had ever seen any third baseman. He bunted again, and again beat it out. McMullen threw his glove away in dismay.

"I'd like to get 3,000 hits before I hang up my spikes. But if I don't make it in the next five years, I won't hang around chasing after them. I know everybody says it, but I'd like to finish on top.

"Right now, I just want to go out there and have fun, let baseball be the little boys' game it's supposed to be. I enjoy playing. I get the feeling that no one can do the things I can, that I can get a hit any time I want. It's a good feeling."

4

# BOBBY ORR

## A Whole New Dimension

Determining "firsts" in sports is easy because revolutionary changes don't happen that often. You can credit Babe Ruth, for example, for turning the home run into a formidable baseball weapon instead of a once-in-a-hundred lucky stroke. Hank Luisetti is considered basketball's first one-handed jumpshot artist, which created a new level for that sport. Notre Dame's Knute Rockne and Gus Dorais are popularly recognized for introducing the forward pass.

In hockey there are Bobby Hull, the first slapshot practitioner, and Jacques Plante, the goaltender who introduced the face mask. However, if you want to name someone responsible for changing the structure of ice hockey, it has to be Bobby Orr. He was the player who turned the game into the explosive style it has today. It is Orr who is the permanent standard by which to judge a defenseman, a skater, a stick-handler, a shooter.

Until a Bobby Orr came along, defensemen were only that: DEFENSEmen. They seldom strayed from their own blue line, being built of sufficient size and girth to stop attackers with their body and knocking them flat if any insisted. They weren't usually fast, but they made up for that by their great strength. They weren't usually fancy puck-carriers, so they concentrated on knocking the puck out of their zone.

Then Bobby Orr was "invented," That meant a rushing defenseman who, when he wasn't performing his normal duties of crunching opponents with body-checks, could also skate, fake, pass, and score—just like a slick forward. Until Orr came along, no National Hockey League defenseman had ever been credited with more than 20 goals a season. Orr topped that mark seven times, including a record 46-goal output in 1974–75.

Other defensemen watched him in awe, then began to imitate—well, try to imitate. Defensemen began to be judged not only on how they kept the other team's pucks out of the net, but also how often they put them in for their own team. They had to learn to stand up at the blue line instead of hanging back in a pure defensive style. They had to practice pursuing pucks behind their net besides just belting the nearest opponent on his backside.

All because that was the way Orr played. And, like Orr, they had to carry the puck, pass the puck, shoot the puck, and in general control the pace of an entire hockey game if they were to be considered a fine all-around defenseman. Whether or not they could, they all dreamed of being able to. Every defenseman growing up on the plains of Saskatchewan or on the streets of Boston imagined himself an Orr.

It is because of Orr that we now call defensemen "offensive defensemen" or "defensive defensemen." A team will usually combine the two styles for each shift if they are lucky enough to possess both kinds. With an Orr, of course, you needn't worry.

Orr was not just another good player. He was an era unto himself, as well as the criterion against which all other hockey players could measure themselves just to see how close to him they weren't. Trying to measure up has ruined some fine talent, too. Ron Andrews, the N.H.L. statistician, once observed: "You can't be a Bobby Orr unless you are Bobby Orr." Many defensemen never discover that fact, much to the disgust of the goalies they leave behind to fend for themselves. Too many offensive-minded defensemen give up more goals than they help their team score.

As one Orr fanatic explained: "Bobby Orr was a swift, powerful skater with instant acceleration, instinctive anticipation, a quick, accurate shot, remarkable composure, an unrelenting ambition, a solemn dedication, humility, modesty, and a fondness for his parents, brothers, and sisters." But unless you have seen Orr in action, it is difficult to comprehend such an enormous scope of talent in one body. When Orr skated, he wasn't just fast; he possessed the unique ability to shift from low to high to highest in an instant, a factor that enabled him to break past opposing players with amazing regularity.

Listen to what opposing players had to say about Orr:

"He can skate rings around me," said Brad Park, one of the game's greatest defensemen *next* to Orr, "as well as all the other defensemen in this league. Because of his speed, he always had an extra split-second to do something extra with the puck."

A Buffalo Sabre defenseman once observed: "When you thought you had Orr cornered and trapped so he couldn't make a pass or pull away from you, all of a sudden he was gone. His fantastic mobility made the difference."

Ken Dryden, formerly one of the game's outstanding goalies, compared Orr's dominance in hockey to that of superstars in other sports: "You can always get an argument," he said, "that this player or that one is the best in football, baseball, or basketball. But as far as Orr was concerned, I don't know if there was another individual who dominated a sport as completely as he did." Dryden added still another facet to Orr's game, saying, "He was on the ice more than half a game, and while he was there he seemed to handle the puck most of the time. He had so many ways of threatening you that players would forget their responsibilities and go to help out a mate trying to stop Orr. That would leave a man open who burned you."

"Let me tell you about this game Orr had against the Oakland Seals," said Gerry Cheevers, a Boston Bruins teammate of Orr. "We're killing a penalty. I wasn't playing, so I watched it from the bench. Bobby drops his glove near the bench. He goes back behind our goal and gets the puck and starts ragging it.

"Then he starts moving. He gets that look in his eyes. He goes faster and faster and faster and pretty soon he's going full-speed and everybody else is trailing him. Then he hits center ice and he bends down and picks up his glove and never loses his stride!

"He puts on his glove, goes full-steam in on the goalie and takes a hell of a shot. He doesn't score, but by that time, who cares? I was standing and cheering, the whole place was standing and cheering—the stands, our bench, even *their* bench. Unbelievable."

Said Emile Francis, an ex-goalie and now a general manager: "Hell, I've seen Orr make a fantastic play on our goal, and when we skate back up the ice, he's there to meet us."

"I played with some great ones," said Don Awrey, a defenseman who was paired with Orr at Boston for seven years. "But no one could go through a team like Bobby. He was electrifying."

How good was Orr?

"The best, the best ever," said Phil Esposito.

"He was in a class above the superstars," added John Ferguson.

What else can you say about Orr? It's all been written and rewritten: the uncanny skating ability; the high-speed moves they call "dekes" in Canada; the peripheral vision; the ability to pick a clear teammate for a pass out of a traffic jam; the booming shot; the slick passes. And, where Orr was concerned, it almost came to be taken for granted.

He was the only defenseman to lead the league in scoring, and he did it twice, 120 points in 1969–70 and 135 points in 1974–75. He won the Norris Trophy as best defenseman eight times, and even in his rookie year, when he missed winning that trophy by a fraction, Harry Howell, who won it, said: "I'm glad I won it now because no one but Bobby Orr will win it for the next twenty years."

Orr won the Calder Trophy, though, for best rookie, and he won three Hart Trophies as most valuable player in the league. He twice was named the best player in the Stanley Cup playoffs (Smythe Trophy), and twice the winner of the Ross Trophy for leading the league in scoring.

In all, Orr won sixteen "best of" awards in the N.H.L.,

more than any other player. Besides holding the defense-man's goal-scoring mark, his 87 assists in a season is the best for defenseman or forward. One record they say is un-touchable: in 657 regular-season games, he tallied 951 points for a 1.39 scoring frequency per game. Orr's statis-tics are a quantum leap ahead of anyone else's who ever played the game.

"He was a star," said Harry Sinden, Orr's former coach in Boston, "from the moment they played the national an-them in the opening game of his rookie season."

His first big-league goal was a blistering 45-foot drive against the champion (as usual) Montreal Canadiens, and it brought him a three-minute standing ovation. He was a regular with the Boston Bruins at the age of eighteen, an all-star defenseman at nineteen, and a legend at twenty—a legend because he was at the same time the sport's best de-fensive and offensive player.

Because Orr is modest, it is difficult to pry from him the analysis of his greatness. One must gain such infor-mation from others who have observed him and played with him. Nearly everyone will agree that Orr was aggres-sive and physical, marvelously self-contained, with an in-stinct perfectly matched to his acquired skills.

Take his skating, which immediately set him apart from all other defensemen and 90 percent of the forwards. It was not just his speed but the deceptiveness of that speed. He had about five different forward gears—and a couple of reverse ones—and he could shift from one to an-other without appearing to change his languid stride.

He was also slippery. Any player coming too close to Orr found that he gave them a little fake, then faded off into an elusive lateral shift or reverse spin before zipping past them in a flash.

As for his speed, it worked like this: He started up the ice with the puck, saw that center ice was momentarily un-inhabited, and suddenly accelerated. By the time he reached the other team's blue line, he was really traveling, but instead of trying to do it all by himself, he fed the puck to a teammate and burst full speed toward the goal.

If everything went right, he was in the clear at the goal mouth, a step behind the confused defense, and when the return pass was whipped back to him from the wing, he collected the puck with one quick motion and shot it into the cage.

"I don't know what I'm going to do until I get there," Orr would say. "I always aim to score, but I never know why or how. Sure, I've gotten lucky goals, caroms off the seat of the pants and things like that. But I freaked out of some I should have had. It evens up, I guess."

Balance was another of Orr's keys. Since he seemed to be controlling the puck for most of the game, the reason was that no one could knock it off him, or, if they came close, he had that outrageous sense of anticipation as well as knowing not only what every player was doing at that precise moment, but also what every player was thinking of doing the next moment.

Balance helped him in fights, too, though Orr will tell you that "the only reason I've gotten into fights on the ice was because I was in a bad mood. And I was beaten, too." But Mike Walton, his teammate, called Orr one of the better fighters in the league. "There are two reasons. First of all, he was so quick. Secondly, he had such a magnificent sense of balance."

Orr was inventive, too, and every new stratagem he pulled out of his hat left opposing players gawking in amazement. He seemed to be devising variations on his variations.

"The most surprising thing about Orr was that he had anything left to surprise you with," said one coach. "You thought you'd seen the ultimate execution of some beautifully subtle idea. Then he would surpass it. His unplanned moves were the most breathtaking of all. Within his area, Orr was a genius."

Ron Greschner, the Ranger defenseman, can attest to that. When he was a nineteen-year-old, Greschner tried to stop Orr's patented end-to-end rush by standing at the blue line. Orr put a one-handed deke on him. Greschner fell flat. Orr then continued in on toward the goal with another defender on his back and put a one-handed backhander on net. The goalie saved, but another Bruin popped in the rebound.

"He can do all that one-handed?" asked Greschner in a bewildered state. "I don't think I want to see what happens when he uses both hands."

Added Brad Park: "When Bobby's on the ice, you're playing against an extra man."

Asked to explain his powerful shot, his deceptive speed, his uncanny passing ability, etc., Orr could only respond in this way:

"To me, hockey was always just a game. If there is a science to it, I don't know what it is. I just went out there on the ice and skated and looked for openings. I didn't know whether my shot was any harder than anyone else's, and I didn't particularly care."

Asked if there was any secret to his unique style of play, Orr said, "I'm not sure that I know. If the talent was there, I'd say it was mostly a case of hard work. I think part of it, maybe, was learning to work with those around me. Nobody can do it by himself all the time. The odds are too great. I've noticed that those teams and individuals who blend their skills the best usually are the ones who win."

"Hard work" to Bobby Orr was probably fun when he was a kid and growing up in the resort town of Parry Sound, Ontario, on Canada's Georgian Bay. When it was summer, young Bobby played a little baseball and golf, but when it was winter, there was only one thing to do: play hockey.

"I got my first skates when I was four," Orr said, "and most of the time, I just did what all the other kids did, play on the ice from early morning until dark.

"We were just kids, though, and sometimes there would be thirty of us chasing after the same puck. But we made up our own games, and we never let the weather bother us. It's always cold in Parry Sound, but even when it got to 40 below, we still played.

"That's where I learned to stick-handle. If you couldn't grab a puck and keep it, you didn't play much and you didn't have much fun."

Almost from the beginning, Orr was able to dominate a hockey game. Before he was ten, he would dance on the ice among the bigger boys, going between them and around them, steering the puck all day, it seemed, until the snow started falling and chased them home.

By the time he was nine and playing with the Peewees, Orr's parents knew they had a prodigy. He skated better than his peers—even better than his older brothers—and he had caught the eye of hockey scouts. It was not until he was fourteen, though, and had advanced through Canada's highly competitive juvenile amateur leagues that he was signed by a professional team.

In those days, a professional team could lock up the services of a talented kid forever if they got him to sign a "junior A" card. When two Boston Bruin scouts saw a skinny kid making even the older boys look bad, they were willing to shell out $2,500 to sign him.

Before he was sixteen, weighing only 120 pounds, his amateur coach sensed that he had a potential star that would make it to the big leagues. The coach took Orr aside one day and said: "Look, kid, there are too many forwards trying to make it to the pros. You'd be better off as a defenseman."

The Bruins were a club that had done poorly for years, and they realized a player like Orr could transform the team's fortunes. Orr, who had acquired an agent to get him a good contract, also realized it. Though the Bruins didn't like it, they finally agreed to give Orr the largest contract a rookie had ever received in the N.H.L.

Orr became a sudden star and a natural leader despite his shyness. He preferred to dress in the trainer's room rather than face the press and talk about himself. Sometimes his own ability embarrassed him.

Don Cherry, his coach at Boston, recalled one game: "The Atlanta Flames were in Boston, and Orr was killing a penalty by going around and around his net. Suddenly, he took the puck down along the boards on the right side. The whole Atlanta team was waiting in the corner, but he went through and put the puck in the net. No one clapped for what seemed like ten minutes. We were all too stunned to react.

"Then Bobby skated back to the bench, his head lowered as if in shame. He was embarrassed because he thought he had embarrassed the Flames. I've been in hockey for over twenty-five years and I've never seen anyone who even comes close to him."

Ask Bobby Orr about his records if you really want to make him squirm. "Oh, I played my position all wrong," he'll say. "A defenseman is supposed to move the puck up for others, but I've always liked to carry it too much. A lot of coaches would say that's just not the thing to do."

Orr did violate most of the accepted methods for playing the game, but he could get away with it because he was Bobby Orr. The "book" said a defenseman plays an opponent's chest and faces him square. Not Orr. More often than not, he played a rushing forward with his back to him.

Some critics would point out that Orr was on the ice for a lot of goals—opponents' goals. And he was, but only because he was on the ice a lot more than anybody else, for the power play, regular shifts, and killing penalties.

Orr might talk more about his "mistakes." He said, "Once in my rookie year I was coming out of our end with the puck and about the time I saw two Rangers in front of me, I heard one of our guys whisper from behind me: 'Bobby, baby, I got a clear shot.' I gave him the puck. But

51

he turned out to be a Ranger player, and he scored easy. Pretty embarrassing, huh?"

But there was no shyness in Orr when it came to his teammates. "From a distance, you might not be able to appreciate Bobby Orr," said Darcy Rota, a forward. "He's maybe the best who ever played this game. Yet, he was so gung-ho, nevertheless. Before the game he would go around to each guy in the dressing room and bang him with his stick, wishing him luck. He was so enthusiastic, so intense, you felt you had to be the same way. And he kept it up on the bench, too."

"It takes luck to reach stardom," Orr says. "Maybe I did react to what was happening on the ice quicker than most players. I don't know. But I never planned my moves. I'd see daylight and I'd shoot. Or I'd spot a teammate open in front of the net and I'd try to hit him with a pass. You don't have time to think. You act and react.

"And I got a few breaks, too. I've scored some decisive goals, especially in the playoffs, but I didn't kid myself. I was lucky."

Ask anybody about Orr today, and you'll probably hear that he was the *unluckiest* player to play the game. Injuries did him in, especially to his knees. He managed to survive the usual multitude of injuries that hockey players suffer in their upper anatomy. Players drove sticks into Orr's back and knees and into his groin so violently that once his shoulder was fractured and another time separated.

His nose, which slants right, was broken six times, and the edges of his mouth were cut five times, deeply enough to require twenty-two stitches one time. "Aah, that's Band-Aid stuff," Orr would say. "You know, I've still got all my teeth."

But at the age of twenty-nine, Orr had had six operations on his knees, and by then, there was nothing between the two bones to act as a cushion. Though he tried, playing twenty games in such a precarious condition, he finally had to give up the game.

One of his last games reminded some people of his early ones, though. "Orr came skating along with his head going in one direction, his shoulders in another, and his hips shooting out a third way, you know how he does it. Well, that night, he came in alone on the two defensemen and gave them such a series of dekes, you know what happened? They crashed into each other and knocked each other down. Orr just walked in on goal with no one around and scored."

Fortunately, the Bruins allowed Orr to play defense and think offense. They permitted a great player to become the greatest by letting him use his instincts in a position for which they were classically not suited. But it made all the difference, for hockey defenses were not designed to cope with an attacking defenseman. One Stanley Cup game serves as a perfect example:

Stationed at the blue line of the opponent, Orr spotted the puck as it came flying out of a mixup of players about twenty feet from the goal. He dashed in, retrieved it, passed it to his teammate, picked up a return pass in front of the goal, and scored.

"Orr did three things wrong on that play," said the rival coach. "First, he did the wrong thing at the blue line when he charged the puck. If it had got by him, the other team would have had a clean breakaway and possibly the winning goal.

"After he knocked the puck over to the other guy, he made another mistake. He should have gone back to the blue line, but he headed for the net. Then he made his third mistake. Instead of lifting the puck over the goalie when he got the return pass, he slid it through the goalie's legs.

"He's the only player I know whose mistakes keep turning out so brilliantly that you're forced to realize they weren't mistakes at all."

If Orr hadn't retired at twenty-nine because of battered knees he might have played for ten more seasons. If you figured he could score 30 goals a year for five years and 20 goals a year after that, Orr would have reached a total of 463 career goals. Giving him a modest 40 assists for each of the ten seasons would give him 400 more assists, which adds up to a career total of 922.

His point total at age thirty-six would have been about 1,385. It is probably safe to say that Bobby Orr could have scored 500 goals and made 1,000 assists if he had continued playing.

Perhaps that is one reason why the public-address announcer in Boston always pronounced his name "Awe."

# 5

# KAREEM ABDUL-JABBAR

## Fantastic "Big-Little" Man

Sometimes it takes a decade or two after retirement for a great player to truly reap the glory he deserves. Sometimes you have to wait until he dies before ironically labeling him an "immortal." But one day, the facts suddenly sink in and the general public will finally declare: Hey, he was the greatest player the game has ever known.

Knowing this is what puts Kareem Abdul-Jabbar in such an extraordinary light. He has already been acclaimed the best "big man" to play the game of basketball, and the remarkable fact remains that he continues to perform while so recognized. In short, Jabbar has become a legend in his own time, a status reserved only for the No. 1 star of a league composed of No. 1 stars. It is one of the rarest and most complimentary attributes anyone can pin on an athlete.

Brilliance can blind the mind's eye. As a fan, you see it, but you don't believe it, partly because its incredibility hasn't registered. Constantly blinded by the 7-foot-2-inch Jabbar, who not only towers over most of his opponents but also weighs 240 pounds and has a standing reach of 9 feet, the basketball world has nevertheless been able to focus on the man's immense talents.

Even as he adds to his unparalleled records, the public has seen fit to pronounce: Yes, Jabbar is the greatest—absolutely.

The legend has had plenty of competition, though. It is not easy to forget the fantastically powerful Wilt Chamberlain, another 7-footer, who scored a record 100 points in an N.B.A. game mostly by muscling the ball near the basket and dropping it through.

No one can demean the overpowering presence of Bill Russell, either, who, though under 7 feet in height, could repulse an opponent's attack by his jumping skills and reflexes for blocking a shot.

And the N.B.A. no longer wants for 7-footers, most of whom end up facing Jabbar and finding they are "boys" in a man's game.

What is it, then, besides his towering height, a body supported by size 16-D basketball shoes and hands that can curl around a basketball as if it were a grapefruit, that make Jabbar the most dominant force in professional basketball?

The secret, the measure of greatness surrounding Kareem Abdul-Jabbar, is his ability to make you forget his tallness. When you watch this man play basketball, you see a "small" man operating around the key like a guard or a small forward, throwing head fakes, feinting with his body, dribbling magically, darting quickly through an opening, and shooting in deadly fashion from the outside perimeters.

"Look at Jabbar's hands, the quickness in the way he bounces the ball," said Wayne Embry, who was general manager of the Milwaukee Bucks when Jabbar was their center and "franchise." "You've probably heard people say that Jabbar wouldn't be playing this game if he were not 7 feet tall. They are wrong. He'd be playing in this league if he were 5-11."

Unlike other centers of great size, Jabbar does not play his position with the plodding style of the behemoth. Not only is he agile and quick, he presents a looming image with his long muscular legs and arms that are sweepingly exaggerated. He is the No. 1 giant in a world populated with giants.

"Kareem's body is as well tapered as any player in the league, regardless of size," claimed Pete Newell, former general manager of the Los Angeles Lakers, which became Jabbar's second professional team. "His leg development is beyond a man of his size. Russell and Willis Reed had great upper-torso development. Chamberlain was probably the strongest athlete I've ever seen, but none of them had the leg development Kareem has."

All right, so the big man can dribble, move agilely, and shoot from anywhere. But how long can he keep it up? According to Phil Johnson, the former Kansas City Kings' coach: "Yes, Kareem can do all those things, yet he still has the stamina and mental attitude to go with the speed and agility. Who stops him? No man alive. You just have to play position—and pray."

Reed, they say, was stronger than Jabbar, but he wasn't as big. Russell might have had the edge with his quickness on defense, but could you trust him at the other end of the court when you needed a basket? As for Chamberlain, he was known as a stationary center, strong on ball-handling and muscle. And, it should be added that he was a prolific scorer *before* the three-second rule was written into the book.

But Jabbar is the moving pivot, with the speed and finesse of a forward. Added Phil Johnson: "If you had to mold a player and say, this is the perfect center, it would be Kareem."

What an arsenal Jabbar brings to a team's offense. Besides getting free most of the time, passing off for easy buckets while drawing two defenders to him, Jabbar plays the game on a mountaintop.

He tosses up a hook shot that arcs so high it's called the "sky hook." He has perfected it so he can sink it with either hand, in close or outside. He has the jump shot to complement the ultimate weapon, his slam-dunk, which brings down the house. Unstoppable.

Defending his own basket, he clogs the whole center area with the wing-spread of two huge eagles. Line-drive shooters have to readjust their style and put the ball up near the ceiling. The opposing center can't match Jabbar's quickness, so he gets rid of the ball before it's batted out of his hands. Any thought of a close-in shot is quickly erased by the incredible flickering hands that surround Jabbar's opponent.

One shot. That's what the other guys get. Up it goes, and unless it's high enough, accurate enough, and quick enough, Jabbar has managed to get a piece of it. If he doesn't and it hits the rim or backboard, kiss it goodbye, the rebounds belong to Abdul-Jumping-Jack-Jabbar.

Often, he won't even allow the shot to reach the basket, preferring to stop it before it begins its downward flight, controlling it with one huge paw and using the other hand to send a long pass downcourt, the start of his team's fast break. When you play with Jabbar, you start thinking fast break when the other team shoots.

"Like picking cherries," his awed opponents call it.

Sometimes, the defensive strategy against a potential Jabbar fast break is to have all five men race down the other end where the ball is supposed to be passed. That only brings the guard out of Jabbar, who lopes down the length of the floor with his island-hopping dribble. Often, he'll continue right on in for a layup. Red faces.

For fifteen years, three with the U.C.L.A. varsity (which captured the national championship each time, winning 88 of 90 games), and eleven in pro ball (where he earns as much as $650,000 a year), Jabbar has proved the game's totally dominating force. Unrivaled in college, six times the N.B.A.'s most valuable player, at the top of the list in scoring, rebounds, assists, and blocked shots, he is the man to stop in every team's strategy book.

Was Jabbar born superhuman? It almost seems so. Before he changed his name from Lew Alcindor, he played an important role on his high school team, Power Memorial Academy in New York City. The record shows that Power played 93 games with Alcindor, who scored a city record of 2,067 points, and they won 92. Near perfection. In college, only two defeats for his club in 90 contests. Near perfection. So what is the word that best describes the next plateau, for that's how Jabbar continues to perform in the N.B.A.? A lot of people are still looking for the word.

When he was born on April 16, 1947, as Lew Alcindor, he weighed 13 pounds and measured 21½ inches. By the time he reached the sixth grade, he was 6 feet tall. One day his teacher glanced up from her desk and asked him, "Why aren't you sitting down?"

"I am sitting down," he replied.

His startling height became an overwhelming factor in his life. Everywhere he went, he was stared at. For anyone growing up, that becomes a problem.

"A very tall person at that age," he said, "fits into a special social category and makes you feel isolated. Most tall boys don't mix and play sports as much as they should."

Jabbar explained that he was 6 feet 8 inches when he got out of grammar school, but by the time he was to feel any sense of isolation, he's already had a strong start in sports.

"I came from a very basketball-oriented community in Harlem," he said, "which also helped me improve. We played in school, but we also played during the summer in playgrounds."

At Power Memorial, Alcindor became a mystery because his coach, wise to the world, kept him from the press and college scouts. His feats were known, but not his beliefs. Everybody knew he was the best high school player in the country, but they knew very little about the person.

One fact became certain, however; he was well aware of his roots. A very good student in high school as in college, Jabbar underwent significant changes in his personality and character his last year at Power. It was no coincidence that it was also the summer of the Harlem riots.

"I was going through this heavy racist thing," he explained, "and I wanted to fight, kick." Soon, he became attached to Malcolm X and eventually decided he wanted to make an intellectual commitment to Islam. When Malcolm X was killed, Alcindor was "an angry black man" who backed the Olympic boycott, converted to the Islamic faith, and changed his name.

As Kareem Abdul-Jabbar, which translates into "noble and powerful servant of Allah," he hoped to bring blacks together by impressing upon black youngsters that even sports figures had a responsibility toward their future. Succeeding at basketball, he says, has opened up a lot of good things in that respect.

Those who recall Jabbar as he was in his days as Lew Alcindor found the enlarged dimensions of his life an important instrument in enlarging the dimensions of his game.

When he first went to U.C.L.A., his chief weaknesses were that he tired quickly and tended to turn away from the basket as the ball left his hands so that he was unable to position himself for a rebound if his shot missed.

Always serious, almost solemn, he worked hard to cure that imperfection, as well as to improve his stamina with a special training program the college trainer had developed for him. He would jump fifteen times in a row, and touch a line on the backboard, 1½ feet away from the basket.

"I didn't expect to grow as tall as I did," he says, "so I learned all aspects of the game, including dribbling. I have been blessed with certain natural attributes. But when a gift is supplied, one must take the time and effort to develop and refine it. Stamina is all a question of being in condition.

"But the mental aspect is also very important. You have to want to be in condition and work at it. Jumping rope has always been a big plus for me."

Stamina and mental preparedness are two of his fine qualities; intensity is another. One year, in a preseason game, Jabbar was playing against Don Nelson of the Boston Celtics (now the coach of the Milwaukee Bucks). In a struggle for the ball, Nelson's finger caught Jabbar in the eye and scratched it. It was the sixth time in his career Jabbar's cornea had been scratched, and he immediately knew the severity and consequences of such an injury: a long convalescence on the bench.

That's when, in complete frustration and anger, Jabbar smashed his right hand against the post that held the backboard. Now, besides a scratched eyeball, he had a badly broken hand. He missed sixteen games, all but three of which his team at the time, the Bucks, lost.

Jabbar is such an imposing figure on the court that rules have been changed to try and limit his potential. Even while a student at Power Memorial, his ability to dominate the game so frightened the National Collegiate Athletic Association (N.C.A.A.) that it outlawed the dunk shot.

Then, long before he was to graduate from U.C.L.A. and enter the pros, the N.B.A. widened the center lanes from 12 to 16 feet and banned offensive goaltending, a fancy name for the way Jabbar grabbed balls right off the rim of the basket and put them in.

But the rules changes only helped Jabbar, noted many a coach. One of them commented: "When Wilt Chamberlain was growing up, the lanes were narrow and he could camp himself underneath the basket. No official counted to three and blew his whistle for a violation. With the widened areas of the key, it wasn't so much a center's game. But since Jabbar had to shoot from farther away from the basket, he developed more shots, including the greatest hook in the game."

Though Chamberlain holds almost every N.B.A. scoring record, it wasn't until he altered his style drastically, emphasizing passing and defense instead of personal points, that he played on his first championship team.

In Jabbar's first seven seasons as a pro, he was named rookie of the year and M.V.P. three times while leading Milwaukee to the league title.

"I don't get a big charge about being the leading scorer," Jabbar has said. "The object of competing is winning. I just try to do what has to be done for us to win. That might be anything at any time—defense, rebounding, or passing. I get satisfaction out of being a team player."

Most centers, coming down the court, don't move the way guards and forwards do; they are only about half as active. But Jabbar moves from the "high" and "low" post outside the basket, from one side of the lane to the other. He even brings the ball down when he has to. He exerts far more energy than most big men. Even when he gets the ball in the post, he uses moves and not just muscle.

"Wilt was predictable," Jabbar says. "You always knew what he was going to do, but he was too strong, and you couldn't keep him from doing it. I learned a lot about defense watching Russell. I would watch the way he would position himself for rebounds and the way he blocked shots."

In a game against the New York Knicks, Jabbar was seen going after Walt Frazier, the Knicks' superdribbler, That astounded a lot of observers, seeing such a tall man trying to flick the ball out of the hands of an artist like Frazier. But Jabbar had the agility to try tricks like that.

"He could be the first 7-foot backcourt man," said Fred Crawford, who grew up in New York with Jabbar and later was his teammate on the Bucks. "He can dribble and make moves no big man ever made before."

To prove his influence on a team as well as the league, a look at the record should suffice. Before Jabbar turned professional, the Bucks had finished last in the Eastern Division of the N.B.A. with a record of 27 victories and 55 defeats. The following season, with Jabbar at center, the Bucks won 56 games, lost 26, and rose to second place.

Not only that but they also increased their attendance by more than three-thousand a game and more than doubled the gate receipts. The team's stock, which was traded over the counter, more than doubled its selling price per share.

When he grew unhappy in Milwaukee, he was big enough to force a trade to Los Angeles. Suddenly, the Lakers were in for a change. Before he arrived, they had finished with a 30–52 won-lost record, the second worst in the league. With Jabbar, the club never finished worse than second.

"Kareem does so much more than anyone can expect of any player," said Jerry West, who was coaching the Lakers at the time. "We just had no business going as far as we did, and Kareem's got to be the explanation. It's a fantastic tribute to his qualities as a man that he could carry a team the way he carried ours. When a great player plays that hard, things happen that just go beyond the limits of the game."

West, a superplayer himself in his N.B.A. days, was able to learn a lot more about his star player than just what he did on the court.

"I guess Kareem fascinates me because I was never able to figure him out before he came to L.A. We played against each other for five years, but he was such a private person, he never said anything to anybody. I used to wonder what he was all about.

"Now, since I've gotten to know him, I think of him as very gregarious, a good talker, a guy with a million interests. He's so well read it's amazing. On the planes, everybody else will be sleeping or listening to music, but there's Kareem with the financial page of *The New York Times*.

"And when you get into conversations with him, he says things that have some meaning. It's not just banter with Kareem."

Jabbar admits he doesn't like to talk basketball, says it bores him. "As long as I express myself adequately playing the game," he said, "there shouldn't be that much left to say."

He is the same way about signing autographs, and kids who have his signature possess one of the rarer names in basketball. He signs a small quota and then stops.

"You know why?" he explained. "Because I remember when I was a kid standing out in front of Yankee Stadium. My toes were all cold and everything, so finally the New York Giants came out, and I got Charlie Conerly's autograph and Andy Robustelli's, too. So what happens? The following Tuesday I didn't even know where the autographs were, and what's more, I didn't even care. That's why I don't like signing autographs."

If a black youth were to ask Jabbar for advice on becoming a star athlete or even a mediocre pro basketball player, he would get a negative reaction plus a lecture on why Jabbar is in the game. Let Jabbar explain it:

"Look, there are about two hundred players in the N.B.A. That's two hundred players out of 200 million Americans. There's only a certain number of people in the country who can do what we do as well as we do it, and the fact that we *can* do it and that people will pay to see it makes other people earn money.

"If you have a piece of the economy," he continued, "you have power. Any man wants power—the power to make life cool for his family and himself, power to do the things he wants to do, right? And basketball is a vehicle to get some of that capital."

Another subject that can annoy Jabbar is his height, especially when it is exaggerated. At times he has been listed as 7 feet 5. "I'm 7 feet 1⅞ inches," he says, "and anyone who says otherwise is being fallacious."

What causes his annoyance, no doubt, is having someone think that his success has resulted from his size alone, rather than the strict work and rare dexterity that have created the elusive quality of his play.

However, when Jabbar appeared on the former television show "Laugh-In," he amazed many of the people who know him with the following routine:

Small blonde girl: "Come on, say it just once."

Jabbar: "Aw, O.K., *fee, fi, fo, fum.*"

Later, he defended the sketch, saying, "I didn't think it was demeaning at all. Contrary to what a lot of people think, I don't have hangups about my height. The thing is, people have made unkind, cruel jokes all my life. I've heard them all and they're not funny. But I'm proud of my height and pleased by it, and it didn't do any harm to do that line for fun."

When paired off against players of his height, the pride that Jabbar claims for being as big as he is comes out for all to see. Against the Bob Laniers, Artis Gilmores, Elvin

Hayeses, Dave Cowenses, Darryl Dawkinses, and Bill Waltons, he is at his spectacular best. He storms out to his position, gnashes his teeth, stomps his feet, and looks menacing. But it's not for doing harm.

"We don't try to hurt each other," he says. "We just try to hurt each other's feelings."

Though, at times, he comes out second best in such excruciating duels, no one ever gets the best of him twice in a row. And over the course of the season, Jabbar will beat the competition by an average of 6 to 10 points, as well as 4 to 5 rebounds, a game.

Walton, who has been compared to Jabbar more than any other player, followed him to U.C.L.A. Both had the same coach, John Wooden, so after some of their epic struggles in professional ball, Wooden might offer the most informed comparison.

"Walton comes closer to making the most of his abilities than Abdul-Jabbar," said Wooden, "but Kareem is the outstanding individual in the game today, possibly the best who's ever played."

Though Jabbar represents the enemy when he plays against New York teams, the basketball fans at Madison Square Garden cheer loudly for the former New Yorker. Even when he also beats their team single-handedly.

"About all you can do is pray," said Joe C. Meriwether, the Knick center, who had the unenviable job of trying to stop Jabbar from doing his thing one night at the Garden. "Kareem gets the ball down low, and you don't want him to shoot the sky hook, so you force him left. So then he just turns around and shoots a sky jumper."

The Knicks put two men on him, but a flurry of shots, baseline hooks, lefty hooks going across the lane, turnaround jumpers, all fell through the hoop like leaves descending to earth. Both his guards fouled out in frustration, and when new men appeared, Jabbar hit the open man so often, the Knicks' coach could only shake his head.

At the other end, he blocked four shots in succession

67

KENNEDY

and altered the direction of a few others. Opponents would dribble past their guards, come up against Jabbar, and keep dribbling into the corner. ("What was I supposed to do?" they'd say later. "Kareem was there.")

"He's just the best there is," said Lou Hudson, a former teammate. "You know, there are a lot of good players on this team, but everyone has to accept a secondary role. The offense is geared to him.

"The trouble other teams have is that Kareem would just as soon get an assist as a basket. That's really what makes him so great."

# 6

# BILLIE JEAN KING

## A Sense of Urgency

For raw power, Margaret Court had more. Virginia Wade's bullet serve is faster. Rosemary Casals could run rings around her. For grace of movement and beauty of swing, Evonne Goolagong wins hands down. And for steadiness, Chris Evert invented the word. But if it came down to one tennis tournament, one final match, one last set or deciding game, Billie Jean King in her prime would be the overwhelming choice to win.

Why Billie Jean? How could a stubby 5-foot-4½-inch woman with 20/400 eyesight dominate such a dynamic group of tennis players over the years? What was the secret that allowed her to capture twenty Wimbledon titles and four United States singles championships on four different surfaces, to be ranked No. 1 nationally seven times and to become the first woman athlete to earn more than $100,000 in a season?

"Attitude," replies the thirty-six-year-old Mrs. King, "plus a sense of urgency that made me work and sweat and hit tennis balls day in and day out forever and love every minute of it."

"Single-mindedness," says her former coach, Frank Brennan. "A pride that drove her to succeed at all costs, and a stubborn will not to be humbled, especially in front of a crowd. She's a ham. The more people watching, the better Billie Jean becomes."

"Ego," adds an opponent. "It's what Billie Jean is made of, and it's what has made her what she is today. Combined with the inexhaustible energy of a marmot, it compels her to become the best in anything she touches."

"Let's face it," Billie Jean insists, "the game of tennis is mental. Anybody at the top can serve an ace, rifle a forehand crosscourt, a backhand down the line, or smash an overhead into oblivion if they practice enough. All the stars can do it.

"It's when you walk out on the court, knowing you and your opponent both have all the shots, that something else must determine the edge. More often than not, it's psychology that takes over, a self-awareness that makes you understand the pressure situations and gives you the confidence to produce the right shot at the key points of the match."

But it has to be almost automatic, instinctive to a player, she believes. "It's like when a big bear chases you in the forest," she says. "You don't stop to figure it out; you just get the hell out of there."

According to Billie Jean, there are certain moments in every match that become the turning points or the keys to winning or losing. It's different every time, but if you know when they occur and if you can raise your game at the right time, you can usually win the match.

"I play better under a pressure situation," she reflects. "I eat it up. I thrive on tension. It raises my game to its supreme height. That's the real reason for my success."

Billie Jean concedes that when she lost to Miss Goolagong at Wimbledon in 1971, she "waited 365 days to get even with Evonne." While waiting, she psyched herself up to a frenzy.

"That's what makes her one of the greatest players in history," Miss Goolagong observes. "She can get herself worked up to the sky. Ask Bobby Riggs about that if you don't believe me."

Bobby Riggs was a Wimbledon and national champion forty years ago and, in the '70s, a champion hustler. When Riggs claimed any man could beat any woman in tennis, he became No. 1 on the male-chauvinist-pig list and a No. 1 target for Billie Jean, a celebrated women's libber. Their climactic Woman-vs.-Man tennis match in Houston's Astrodome for hundreds of thousands of dollars and a TV audience of 40 million people created more pressure, tension, and urgency than Billie Jean ever imagined.

"That night in 1974," exclaims Billie Jean, "was not only a magnificent spectacle, but the culmination of the second phase of my career. I had already won the fight to become the No. 1 woman player in the world. Now came the battle for women's equality.

"It really came home to me hard, that if I lost to Riggs, much of what we women had won for ourselves might go right out the window. I'd sensed it before, but this time I knew the match was one of the big three in my life—the others were against Maria Bueno in the 1966 Wimbledon final and against Chris Evert at Forest Hills in 1971—in each case where a defeat would just about erase everything that I'd done before."

In an atmosphere that would have rivaled a circus with balloons, bands, noise, gamblers, and clowns, Billie Jean was in her element. "I loved it," she says. "Just the way a tennis crowd ought to be, everywhere. No holds barred. I doubt if there was a neutral person in the whole Astrodome."

The scores were 6–4, 6–3, 6–3 for the historic match, and when it was over, Billie Jean said: "I'm sure a lot of players who watched the match were convinced they could beat Riggs, too, so what's the big deal? Well, sure they could beat him—on their home-club court with three people watching. But let 'em try it before 40 million people and I think things would be different."

The key moments of the match, according to Billie Jean, included: "The first game because it set the tempo of the whole match"; picking the right time to go to the net, "for when I succeeded, it threw his whole thinking off," and overcoming fear. "Champions are afraid to lose," she added, "when most others are afraid to win."

But she didn't discount technique, either.

"If you don't have the shots or the ability to put the ball where you want it at the time you want to," she says, "then it doesn't matter how much confidence, stubbornness or will power you've got. You're not going to do the job."

Billie Jean has always seemed to own a sufficient supply of confidence to go with her ability. In early childhood when her parents persuaded her to switch from football and softball to the more ladylike pastime of tennis, she made the brash prediction that she would be No. 1.

"Secretly, I was terrified," she admits. "It's bad enough when you silently think about becoming No. 1, but when you tell everybody, you suddenly feel that perhaps you're not going to make it."

Says her mother, Betty Moffitt: "Billie Jean knew what she wanted in life when she was only eleven. Many children don't know what they want to do with their lives in their twenties. When she said she was going to win at Wimbledon some day, I told her: 'Well, if you think so, that's fine. Why not?' Maybe I encouraged her because I thought it was possible, too."

Devoted parents help, in any case. Her mother took Billie Jean to a park every day it didn't rain. When Billie Jean's brother, Randy, began playing Little League baseball, she took one to the park to play tennis and the other to the baseball diamond to play baseball. Randy, of course, went on to become a major-league pitcher with the San Francisco Giants.

"Weekends I packed a lunch for them," Mrs. Moffitt says. "Billie Jean would play tennis from eight o'clock in the morning till dark. She particularly liked to play singles because it meant more running and competition."

Billie Jean won her first trophy when she was twelve. From that moment, the treasures from winning tennis tournaments piled up until they had to be stored away in closets.

"I knew she'd become a champion just by seeing her reactions to the tournaments she lost," Mrs. Moffitt says. "She took her wins happily, and when she lost, she didn't cry or become upset. She analyzed her game and then would say: 'Gee, Mom, I know why I lost. I shouldn't have hit so many balls to her forehand.' Some players lose and never know why. Billie Jean always found the right reason and then practiced until she overcame the problem."

Billie Jean practiced so hard she wore out a pair of tennis shoes a week. Once she practiced serves for several hours and came home with a hole in a pair of brand-new sneakers. After that, her parents wrapped the toes of her shoes with adhesive tape so they would last longer.

"She wanted to become a champion so much," said Mrs. Moffitt, "she walked three miles to school and three miles back again in her senior year in high school. She knew it would take more than just determination and that conditioning was important."

In this respect, Billie Jean was motivated by Rev. Bob Richards, the former Olympic pole-vault champion, who was pastor of the First Church of the Brethren, a few blocks from the Moffitt home. Richards baptized Billie Jean when she was ten, and after Sunday services, before she headed for the tennis courts, he would emphasize to her the importance of physical fitness.

Suddenly, her training became intense. For about seven years she learned the art from Clyde Walker on the public courts, then under the tutelage of Alice Marble, one of the great women players, and later from Frank Brennan, a taskmaster who taught her not only what she was doing right and wrong, but also why certain things worked and others didn't. All of this culminated in a three-month crash course at the hands of Mervyn Rose, a former Australian Davis Cup star, who combined physical endurance and technical craftsmanship into a thinking woman's game.

The results of this exhausting course are written in the record book as well as her own book, *Tennis to Win*, in which she recounted:

"Unless you happen to be extremely gifted, there is no such thing as instant gratification in tennis. Most of us can tee up a golf ball and hit it with a club, maybe not very far or very straight, but at least with some immediate tangible result. Or most of us can take a bowling ball and after a few tries knock down a few pins.

"But hitting a moving object while you yourself are moving takes a pretty fair amount of coordination. And more yet is needed to hit a ball back across a net, 36 inches high at its lowest point, into a singles court that is 39 feet long and 27 feet wide."

Another obstacle Billie Jean had to overcome was her physique. Though born with quickness and coordination, she usually gave away a lot to her opponents in the tale of the tape. Margaret Court was 6 inches taller; Martina Navratilova outweighed her by 30 pounds, and Virginia Wade, lankier and taller, possessed the sinewy arms and legs of an athlete.

"But compare us on the court," Billie Jean will say. "Evonne's forehand is the same as mine. But I apply myself to the backhand better. Maneuverability, she's smoother. But net game, I'm steadier.

"Compare me with Court. She was long, bigger physically with a better reach, better first serve, more power. But she wasn't so good under pressure and not as good in the hands nor in speed and agility.

"Rosie Casals is fast, no doubt about it. But the secret of speed is in the first two steps. I'm pretty quick off the mark. In school, I always won the short races, against boys or girls.

"As for Virginia, her serve is terrific. But you win on your second serve. And mine is the best.

"I guess I'm the shortest person to win so much, though. Most champion players have been 5 feet 7 or more. My legs are my strength, short as they are. My upper body is the weak part. But when you're small, you must put the ball away quicker. You have to. If you're small, you better be a winner."

Adds Arthur Ashe, "She's a hell of an athlete. That's

the most important thing for a woman. Forget the strokes; if you can move on your feet, you can win."

And you'd better be in shape, Billie Jean adds. "Look at Martina and Chris. Martina had it all over Chris in size, strength, quickness, and even coordination. But who won most of the time? It's how Chris applied herself. It's psychology and how you adapt that count, not size."

Billie Jean can cite the two most difficult drawbacks in her sporting life: weak eyes and bad knees.

"I've had to wear glasses since I was twelve," she says. "Nearsighted. I tried contact lenses for three years but gave them up. They irritated me. If I wore them six hours one day, I couldn't wear them at all the day after. But I still see the ball well, which amazes me. My reflexes make up for it, plus footwork and balance."

As for her knees, she's had several painful operations as well as a complete rebuilding of those vital joints. "Deterioration of the patella, some big fancy medical term," she remembers. "That set me back. I had to recover first and then play myself back into competitive shape. It was rough."

The secret is to stay in shape, she says. Her ideal playing weight is 138 pounds, but she tries to keep her diet low in fats, at 10 percent or under. "Ice cream is the devil in my eating program," she admits.

Asked to analyze her own play, Billie Jean says she is stumped. "It's difficult for a player to analyze herself when she rarely gets a chance to see herself play. I'd love to see me on film. If I could watch myself play, I could figure out how to beat me.

"When I first started out in tennis, I would rather play artistically than win. You get more satisfaction that way, but when you lose, however artistically, you don't get the privilege of going out there and performing the next night, too. That was the hardest thing for this little girl to learn.

"I guess flexibility may be the key to the whole business of winning when you reach the top. I am a more flexible player than the others. I'm also very emotional. I can give 100 percent. I can set a goal, such as Wimbledon, and get myself psyched up. When I have a meaningful goal, I'm tough to beat."

She has always been that way, according to her parents. She wasn't temperamental on the court or at home, they said, but she talked to herself on the court just as she does in tournaments today.

"It's self-criticism or maybe she's giving herself a pep talk," explains Mrs. Moffitt. "She told me more than once it's a healthy outlet for her, that she'll just explode if she can't talk to herself a bit. 'I'm not tranquil enough to keep a poker face,' she's said. Of course, she may have become more temperamental than she was because of all the pressures of big-time tennis."

There were other pressures, too. Her dealings with organized femininity, her role as Mother Tennis in leading the women's tour out of anonymity, her own magazine, *WomenSports*, her marriage with Larry King on her own terms, her abortion, her complete faith in World Team Tennis, her promotional appearances, interviews, and television shows, and finally, her retirement and unretirement.

When she was little Miss Moffitt, Billie Jean was giving out signs that smacked of equal rights. One day when she was thirteen, she said to her mother: "Men beat women at tennis because they play a different type of game. So I'm going to pattern my game after men. I'm going to learn to play the net."

This radical departure from the demure women's style of graceful strokes from the backcourt area brought instant criticism. It simply wasn't the traditional woman's game, and in those days, any departure from the norm, especially the sexual norm, caused attention.

But she kept at it, and it seemed the men's attacking game came easily for her. She began to pattern herself after Tony Trabert and Pancho Gonzales, who were two of the more noted net-rushers of her day. There were few women to idolize.

"Being a girl was not the only thing I had to fight," she says. "I was brought up to believe you had to become well-rounded to succeed. It took a while for me to question that concept and ask: 'Who says we have to be well-rounded? The people who aren't good at anything, that's who.' When I understood that, I could really try to be special."

One of her biggest tradition-busting roles was as head of the women's-liberation movement. It came slowly, but it came naturally. Explains her husband, Larry King: "Billie Jean is for equality of opportunity for women. She didn't think very highly of the feminists at first. She thought they were a bunch of radicals burning bras. But she does believe every woman should have the opportunity to develop her potential, just as she has done."

Look at Billie Jean's personal life if you want to see a liberated woman. She's free of domesticity. She doesn't cook. She doesn't clean house. She doesn't entertain. In fact, she has virtually no home life.

An apartment in San Francisco, an apartment in New York, it matters little. There's an empty refrigerator in either place, save for whatever beverages they've left. Apartments are to store clothes in, flop when you have to stay overnight, and a place to pick up the mail.

"We're usually out," says Larry. "We eat out, travel, and live out of suitcases. Unless we're near our parents' houses, we keep on the move." It's a strange life, a strange marriage, but it's what they both seem to want.

"Even when we're in the same city and Billie Jean is playing in a tournament, we are separated by obligations," admits Larry. "For Billie Jean, there is practice, getting her rest, promotional activities and so forth, as well as the tournaments. Meanwhile, I'm traveling about working on a dozen things myself."

Billie Jean and Larry met at Los Angeles State College and got married shortly after. It took a special sort of man.

Billie Jean was the star of the family, of course, but Larry was content to remain out of the spotlight. Handsome, bright, and hard-working, he devoted himself to his wife's career, becoming her agent, manager, adviser, legal aid, and anything else she needed. He is also a fine tennis player.

Three years after they were married, Billie Jean became pregnant. Again, Larry agreed with Billie Jean that a baby would only interfere. She'd have to give up tennis—and all the fringe benefits that went with it. She decided to get an abortion.

"We've never regretted that decision," she says. "We still want to have children, but we want them to have a life that would be fair to them. Right now, we're happy living as we are. We don't find being apart all that troublesome. We're both caught up in a cyclone of activity and we've come to enjoy it. This is our way of life.

"I guess it all depends on what you consider a good definition of marriage. As for us, if both parties are happy, then it's good. I think we're both happy. Tennis is our world right now."

Even in their common cause, World Team Tennis, they rarely crossed paths. They both helped get the league off the ground, she as a player and a coach; he as a founder and president of the team in New York.

Nearly everybody said the W.T.T.'s novel methods would not work, and when Billie Jean heard remarks like that, it drew her greatest ire. Though many of the best ideas stemmed from Larry's fertile imagination, the fire and zest came straight from Billie Jean. Despite its ultimate collapse in 1978 because of huge money demands by the spoiled top echelon of men's tennis players, World Team Tennis wouldn't have lasted one year, much less six, without the Kings.

It must have hurt, that failure, but you'd never know it looking at Billie Jean. Success is forever evidenced in her

80

expression, but never failure. She once explained that, saying:

"If you want to be the best, you must never let anyone know what you really feel. You see, they can't hurt you if they don't know."

At other times, however, she will reveal a little bit of disgust, or maybe it is disappointment, at seeing how easy it has been for the latest crop of women players to make it to the top and the big money.

"I wish I could be a kid again sometimes," she says, "and come along and have it all organized for me. Recognition is so easy today, but then, no matter how good it gets, I know I've experienced the real things no one else will. I get most of my gratification just seeing the changes in the sport. I don't feel I have to be responsible anymore."

All those people who once thought Billie Jean King came on too strong, prejudged her as "that tough dame," seem to have mellowed now. Maybe they have; *she* certainly has.

"Yes, even now when I read some of those things that I was supposed to have said once, I start to think that fire must have come out of my ears. I guess I've changed. People tell me now when they meet me that I'm not at all what they thought I'd be, not tough and bitter as the reports had it."

In fact, a national magazine held a poll recently among its readers to see who was the most admired woman in the world. Never had an athlete even come near the top ten, but who came in No. 1 this time? Billie Jean King. The late Golda Meir came in second.

Said the poll's director: "We were stunned. This was a tremendous departure from past surveys. There is something going on out there, with young girls, especially. There are new heroines, but not the high lamas of feminism.

"It seems to be important that Billie Jean did it all on her own, just her and that tennis racquet."

As Billie Jean theorizes: "Life is like a tennis match;

there are so many ups and downs. You can be down to where you think there's no way possible you can win a match. But you just keep trying step by step and finally you win.

"You've got to have the right attitude. Give me attitude over style any day. In the long run, that beats out a great serve, a fantastic net game, mobility, anything."

# 7

# JULIUS ERVING

## Improvisation in Flight

L et's create the ideal basketball player. He should be tall enough to slam-dunk a ball into a basket 10 feet high, yet not so tall he can't maneuver like a swift-moving guard. Give him springy legs to counter the 7-footers, yet still beat an agile forward to a rebound. Let him have the shooting eye of an eagle and the feather touch of a safecracker-turned-dribbler. Add the body control of a contortionist, accompanied by a brain so nimble he can change intentions in midair. Mix in a sixth sense to unerringly head for the ball a split second before his man passes or lets go a shot.

Make him a leader, too, respected by his teammates as well as the fans. Supply him with hamhocks for hands to palm a ball as if it were a grapefruit, plus huge feet for balance as well as to rocket him above a crowd from a standing position. Finally, sprinkle in a magical kind of uniqueness that will make many of his moves so spectacular they cannot be duplicated.

Name him Julius Erving and call him Dr. J, the man experts have termed the most exciting player ever to have set foot upon a basketball court.

"To me," said Billy Cunningham, the Philadelphia 76er coach and former All-Star, "he's the greatest talent I've ever seen. He has the flair for the game the way Bob Cousy and Elgin Baylor did."

Says Kevin Loughery, his coach with the Nets: "Pound for pound, Julius is the greatest and most exciting player in the game. He creates. It just flows out of him. His greatness is in his big hands. There are several pros with hands as large, but none have his size, strength, and sensitivity. If he can get a couple of fingertips on the ball, he will control it."

Yes, one big secret is in the hands. The basketball looks tiny when Erving holds it. He can grab a missed shot with one of those huge paws and pluck it away from taller, bigger players. He can seize a ball one-handed off the bounce and take off for a slam-dunk or stop suddenly and make a quick 15-foot shot. The defense never really knows what he's going to do.

Erving is the first to admit it. "My hands are my strength," he says.

"I remember this skinny, bony kid," said Kareem Abdul-Jabbar, "when he first showed up at the New York City playgrounds. We measured hands. His were bigger. He played one-handed even then, and he stuffed over everybody."

Erving says it's not only his hands but his legs that contribute to his ability, plus the fact that he's "a student of the game."

"Having big hands helps," he says, "but nothing I do on the court is really new."

New to *him* is what he means, for he tried all his tricks out in the Rucker Playground League a long time ago when he was a kid. And he was doing it free in those days.

Give him an audience or an important game, and Erving shines even more brightly. A few years ago during an All-Star game between the old A.B.A. and the N.B.A., a ball was hurled downcourt to Erving, who was then an A.B.A. forward. Walt Frazier of the Knicks was trailing him. Quickly, Erving slammed the ball to the floor, brought it behind his back, accelerated at the foul line, soared above Frazier, and slammed the ball through the basket.

Watching was Dave DeBusschere, who said in wonderment: "I've never seen a move like that. The guy kept going up and up. Amazing."

DeBusschere, who became the commissioner of the A.B.A. after retiring from the Knicks, also saw Erving score on a shot made with his body suspended behind the backboard and his right arm extended beneath the backboard and parallel to the rim. DeBusschere fell out of his seat. "Whenever I see Erving play, I come out of my seat," he said. "He has extreme quickness, and his presence on the floor carries respect and leadership. His every acrobatic move blends with the chemistry and makeup of his team.

No one has ever stopped him, and I doubt they ever will. He's the best forward in the game."

Unlike most forwards or centers, Erving is neither skinny nor muscular at 195 pounds. A shade under 6 feet 7 inches, he is about an inch shorter than the average forward in pro basketball.

But he has long arms and those huge hands and feet— he wears a size 15 sneaker and size 13 gloves—which no doubt contribute to his extraordinary body control and the ability to shift the ball from his right hand to his left before he lets it fly from somewhere behind his ear.

Not only are his feet big, but his legs are long, though his great stride hides his speed so that he often lopes right by a defensive man who has not perceived it. Once this happens, he is almost certain to score, even if another man drops off to defend against him. This is because, while moving, he can do almost anything from the floor, and his control in the air defies description.

Erving's ability to hang in the air longer than other players allows him to make decisions at the height of his jump. If he has no shot, he will drop off a pass to a teammate. Or he may lean away from a defender and reach in with one long arm to bank the ball off the backboard. If his path is blocked—usually by two opponents—he simply drops the ball to an unguarded teammate.

This is what electrifies basketball crowds, who think they have seen it all. When he accelerates at the foul line, rockets off the ground and glides over defenders, or picks the ball out of the air as if it were a baseball, he leaves crowds dumbstruck. With a running start, Erving can leap from behind the foul line, some fifteen feet from the basket, and slam-dunk the ball. Leaping, he can reach over twelve feet from the floor.

"Creativity flows out of him," raved Lou Carnesecca, the St. John's University coach who also coached the Nets and Erving. "He possesses great imagination. Every night he upstages himself. You can talk about this guy like a poet, an artist, a great dancer. He is all three on the basketball court."

Adds an opponent: "There's really no way to stop, I mean really stop Julius. You just run him up and down the court, take away the baseline and pray that he gets tired. But he'll still get his 30 points!"

But points don't begin to tell the story why thousands of knowledgeable fans storm the gates to see Erving play. It's the manner in which he scores that keeps them coming. Said one fan: "His leaps and bounds to the hoop are so sweet, I wish they'd give at least a half a point for the move alone."

Erving will not deny he's unique. "My primary difference," he says, "is what I do outside of playing fundamental basketball. I have the ability to score in many ways, inside, outside, and while contested. When it's my turn to solo, I'm not about to play the same old riff."

Yet, he claims he doesn't try to be the hot dog, only that it comes naturally. "It's not something premeditated," he insists, "it's just the way I play ball. Some people say I make them feel good when they see me play. I make a note of it and thank them, but I can't come back and say, 'I intended to make you feel that way.'

"No, sometimes when I start a play I never know if I will be able to do what I would like. But I always go ahead and try. I guess it's sort of like daring to be great. And if it works, fine. If it doesn't, well, the team is always behind me. The coach is behind me. Next time, I just try something else."

Erving's best performances have a certain rhythm in them. It is his habit to save his incredible moves until after the first quarter. "I don't like to get into the offense too quickly," he explains. "I prefer for the guards to get into it first. That way I can determine the flow and my best course of action. Then I can let the game flow toward me. By the second quarter I'm ready to start swooping. But it's important for me to go with the flow and not force it."

The best example of this theory was seen in the final championship series of the A.B.A. Merger with the N.B.A. was just around the corner, and the league, its players, and the two best teams, New York and Denver, wanted to prove they belonged with the best of them. Julius Erving of the New York Nets was one of those players.

As was his custom, he waited till the second quarter to operate against the Denver Nuggets. He had scored but 4 points while he studied the situation. Then suddenly, he poured in 13 points, some of them 360-degree helicopter turnaround slam-dunks that had him flying in the stratosphere. He created such a vacuum, the guys on the bench said, it cracked their ears.

"Why not stuff it?" Erving says. "That's the best way I can see to get the bucket. Some people call it a show, but I've been doing it all my life, and I say when something works, don't change it."

In that game, Erving went on to score 31 points, grab 19 rebounds, hand off for 5 assists, block 4 shots, and steal the ball 5 times in the Nets' 112–106 victory. But that was considered ho-hum compared with the rest of the series. In five games, he scored a total of 195 points, averaged 13.2 rebounds, blocked 9 shots, and stole the ball 13 times.

"A lot of players have his physical talent and tools," said Al Skinner, a former teammate. "In Doc's case, he combines those with a heart, a mind, and dedication like no other player I know. Sure, he has big hands and God-given jumping ability, but it's that dedication of his that gives him such greatness."

While many of his opponents would like to stop and applaud Erving's heroics against them, they save their feelings till after the game. Said David Thompson, Denver's star: "Julius is the greatest. He used to be my idol, but no more. It's pretty hard to idolize a guy you're playing against. I have to keep reminding myself not to stop and watch him."

Though a lot of people think Dr. J was born, not made, he quickly sets them right. "You have to work at being quick. There are guys who can sprint 100 yards in 10 seconds, but they can't do that on the basketball court. It's something that takes developing.

"Body control comes with hard work. You slow down on your opponent, let him catch up, then you make him freeze by accelerating around him. That's when quickness counts."

Then he goes on and explains how he "learned to be trickier" than bigger guys: "I experimented a lot at first. I watched other guys and saw what they did in emergency situations. Then when I practiced, I worked on ways to take advantage of my advantages. I set no dimensions. I decided not to limit myself, and I found I could do anything that I had ever seen anybody else do—except spin the ball on the end of my finger. I could never do that. But you can't use that in a game anyhow."

Erving has been called the only player in basketball who is capable of playing all three positions—forward, guard, and center. The guards are usually the quickest and the best ball-handlers. Erving is quick and a good ball-handler. The forwards are good shooters and rebounders, and Erving shoots and rebounds well. Centers are big and strong, but Erving can jump so well he can overcome their height and width.

In his book, *The Legend of Dr. J*, Marty Bell describes a game that illustrates Erving's tremendous versatility. It was the final game of the 1973 A.B.A. season, with the Nets playing the Denver Rockets and needing a win to clinch first place. After three periods the Nets led, 77–76, and Erving had 31 points, mostly on outside shooting.

"The fourth quarter seesawed back and forth," Bell wrote, "and Julius didn't score for the first six or seven minutes. Then he took over. He started going to the basket, making one shot after another. He scored four baskets in a row and passed off to teammate Brian Taylor for an easy layup for a fifth. But the Nets still led only 98–96 with less than two minutes left. Erving came down the floor again and hit an off-balance 15-foot jump shot for a 100–96 lead.

"He took a rebound of a missed Rocket shot and dribbled the ball out through a crowd of hands that reached for it. Instead of continuing unmolested to the hoop, he pulled up short at midcourt and dribbled around for a few seconds to kill time on the clock. With ten seconds left on the thirty-second clock, he went to the hoop for an acrobatic layup that put the Nets ahead, 102–96.

"The Rockets took the ball out of bounds, and guard Ralph Simpson dribbled downcourt. A Net tapped the ball from behind Simpson and it rolled on the floor toward the Rocket basket. Julius and Denver's Al Smith took off in a foot race to the ball, and both dove head first at it, sliding along the floor, scraping their bodies along the way. The ref called a jump ball.

"The Rockets controlled the tap and worked the ball into 6–10 Dave Robisch for a short-range shot. Robisch turned to shoot, and Julius went up and knocked the ball back at Robisch. The ball bounced on the floor and ten players dove for it. Julius came out of the pack with the ball and dribbled away the last thirteen seconds of the game.

"Julius had scored 12 of his team's last 14 points and assisted on the other 2. He finished the night with 43. He had blocked shots, rebounded, and dove to the floor after the ball. Shoot, dribble, pass, rebound, and play defense. Erving had done them all. The complete ballplayer playing the complete game under the most important circumstances."

To best understand how Dr. J's fabulous style came about, you have to understand the past of Julius Erving. Poor and fatherless as a child, he learned about self-reliance early, and the importance of financial security. Even today, he says, "I think the function of professional athletics is to make money."

When Erving was born, his mother was a cleaning woman supporting two other children in a low-income housing project. When Erving was three, his father left home, and it was his mother who had to provide not only the income, but the inspiration for the family.

"He was never a happy child," noted Erving's mother, who is now Mrs. Callie Lindsey. "He always had to listen, and he didn't give anyone cause to dislike him. He was smart and deep-thinking. But he always liked to make money."

When he turned ten, Erving joined a Salvation Army basketball team in a youth center. That was where he met his first big influence in the game, a coach named Don Ryan, who took an interest in poor youths, especially those from broken homes.

Said Erving: "After playing with the Salvation Army team, I came to see that basketball represented an avenue of getting out and seeing things. The more I saw, the more I wanted to see."

At one time, Erving said, basketball was his only es-cape. "Many times when I was growing up, things would get off on the wrong foot at the house, and I'd go down to the park and play ball all day. When I came back, the trouble which had happened at home was the last thing on my mind. It freed my head."

When he was thirteen, his mother had remarried and the family moved to Hempstead, L.I., where Erving found a "neighborhood playground of green cement" and began to practice regularly. There is a sign still there that says: "This Is Where Julius Erving Learned the Game of Basketball."

When Erving enrolled at Theodore Roosevelt High School, the coaches, Ray Wilson and Earl Moseley, knew all about him. Though he was 6 feet 3, lightning quick, and a superb jumper, they brought him along slowly.

92

Then in his final two varsity years, he became one of the most spectacular performers in the state. Said his coach, "Julius always personified class—even as a high school kid, which was not easy to do and still be one of the guys. He never asserted himself by being brash or loud or lewd. I never remember seeing him in a fight or an argument. Most of the kids always wanted to show they were the best with their fists.

"Julius could always assert himself by creating a move."

It was at Roosevelt High that Erving received part of his now legendary nickname, Dr. J. "I had a friend," he said, "who had a habit of arguing a point and going on to lecture the person he was arguing with. So I called him 'the Professor.' After that, he started calling me 'the Doctor.' It had something to do with the saying, 'He has more moves than Carter has pills.' "

The "J" part was added later when Erving reported to the Virginia Squires in 1971. "There were a lot of people there with nicknames like 'Doc' or 'Doctor,' so Willie Sojourner, a teammate, began calling me 'Dr. Julius' to distinguish me from the others. Finally, the public-relations man came up with 'Dr. J.' "

Erving spent three years in college at the University of Massachusetts before turning pro when he was unexpectedly offered a contract by the Squires of the A.B.A. Al Bianchi, his first pro coach, admitted he had been a bit leery at signing so inexperienced a product as Erving. "He was an unknown quantity," Bianchi said. "I didn't know he'd be great. In fact, I was edgy about the whole deal—until I saw his hands."

But once Erving got on the court and did his thing, there was no doubt in anybody's mind. "We got one here," said Bianchi. "You don't forget seeing a talent like that for the first time. It mesmerizes you. He's got a very special chemistry. He has gone on to surpass everyone who ever played the game."

Other players on other teams had their reservations about Erving, too. They'd heard all these marvelous things about him, and the word-of-mouth spread fast. But basketball players won't believe until they see for themselves. Said one: "You hear all these things, but you wait till you play against him. I mean, they were saying this guy could go higher than Elgin Baylor, and Baylor was my idol, man. So I get to guard this phenom just to see. Man, let me tell you, I was asking for help in no time. He was going right by me. How he could stretch and lean! One-on-one, you could only foul him or let him go. I'd never seen anyone play his position better."

That first year in the A.B.A., Erving maintained his consistency by averaging 27 points and 16 rebounds a game. His spectacular moves astonished opponents, encouraged teammates, and won the allegiance of fans. In the playoffs, Erving raised his game to an unbelievable pinnacle, tallying 53 points, making 21 of 28 shots from the field, grabbing 14 rebounds, and handing out 6 assists.

His teammate, Adrian Smith, was wide-eyed, saying: "When they come to write about the greatest basketball games ever played, Julius Erving's performance tonight will rank up there with the very best. I have seen Jerry West, Oscar Robertson, and the other greats, but I have never seen anyone play better than Erving did for us tonight."

When the New York Nets had Dr. J, they built their entire offense around him. He would come out away from the basket to meet his guards two-thirds of the way downcourt, then one would pass him the ball. Once he had it, his team would clear out a side for him, the four other players moving to the left or right and leaving the other side of the court open for him to begin his routine.

"I watch players, all players," Erving explained. "I watch them on television, at college games, in the playground—you can learn from anybody. Even now I'll be watching a game somewhere and I'll see somebody do something I've forgotten, some little move, maybe. I'll practice it a little and I've got it back, and when the right situation comes along, against some player, maybe I've got a little edge I didn't have before."

Loughery adds another element to his greatness: "Erving is not only the best and most exciting forward in pro basketball, he's also a leader. I mean a *real* leader. He just does more and more. It isn't just the points and the rebounds and the passes; it's the way he does it. I [used to] see something different every night. And off the court, he's one of the nicest guys you'd ever want to meet."

Billy Paultz, a former Nets center, agreed, saying: "Julius is not at all like the stereotype of the spoiled superstar. A lot of superstars think they can take off from practice and loaf now and then on the court. But not Doc. His attitude has a great influence on the team."

If Erving has an idol, it is Bill Russell, the former star center with the Boston Celtics. "I met him in college," Erving stated, "and I found I could relate to him instantly. He talked about school and having kids, and he wanted me to know that in life we have a lot of opportunities, but the ones who advance must recognize them quickly and take advantage of them. It's a form of optimism, and I've always remembered that."

Erving especially practices such philosophy in a game. "When I'm playing and a guy plays dirty and tries to hurt someone, it gets me. That's your career they're fooling with, you know. When a guy tries that on me, I pay him back by embarrassing him."

Erving has always had pride. Instead of fighting, he just slams the ball to the ground, goes to the hoop, and soon everybody knows who's the boss.

"He's so reliable and calm," says his wife, Turquoise. "He never gets mad, and if I get angry, he settles me right down. He's the sweetest, most down-to-earth guy you'll ever meet."

In the A.B.A. or the N.B.A., where he now plays a team-concept role for the Philadelphia 76ers, Erving has always been perfectly suited to a game that constantly evolves. Whether driving for the basket in his fluid, stream-lined style or hanging in the air as if held up by guy wires or simply passing off the ball with a deft finger, Erving epitomizes the grace and beauty of basketball in its ultimate state.

Oh, he does have one weakness. He can't shoot with his feet.

# 8

# PELE

## Computer-like Coordination

Pele has lived to see his name become synonymous with greatness, success, humility, and even perfection.

"Pele" is a simple word. Probably because Pele, the nickname of the world's premier soccer player, is a simple man. But this simple man simply rewrote the record book. You want figures? Pele scored 1,281 goals in his lifetime. That averages out to practically a goal a game for twenty-two years of professional playing. If you're more familiar with baseball, that's equivalent to hitting a home run in every major-league game you ever played.

You want achievements? Pele helped his team (Santos, in Brazil) win every championship it sought. The greatest prize in soccerdom is the World Cup, and when Pele played for the Brazilian national team, it captured the World Cup three times, a feat no other country can match. In fact, Brazil got the cup for keeps following its third triumph in 1970.

You prefer monetary comparisons? Pele earned more money than any salaried athlete in the history of sports. Even when he was far past his prime and had announced his retirement from the game, the Cosmos (of the North American Soccer League) thought enough of his skills to bring him back for three more years by paying him $4 million.

Maybe you're more impressed by names. Before he retired again, Pele had played in eighty-eight countries, visited with two Popes, five emperors, ten kings, and one hundred and eight other heads of state. When he came to the United States to play for the Cosmos, soccer was a struggling, minor sport here that attracted mostly youngsters and foreign-bred fans. Before he quit, however, stadiums around the country were packed with screaming spectators, often more than showed up for football or baseball games. Pele had turned soccer into another major sport just by walking on the field.

There were many other marvelous soccer players performing before Pele arrived. Soccer fans were aching to see the sport thrive in this country as it does all over the world.

But it took Pele to accomplish what nobody else had. It took his graciousness and sincerity, his "divine gift from God"— as he calls it—plus a marvelous physical dexterity to put the game over the top. People wanted to see Pele first, soccer second. But still, today soccer is big-time.

Was Pele a god sent to popularize the game? Let's examine those abilities that made Pele the king of the most popular game on earth. The first thing you'd observe is that Pele was just average in size, standing 5 feet 8 inches and weighing 160 pounds. But don't let that fool you. Pele would glide through and around his opponents like a jaguar. Said an opponent in admiration: "Pele is unbelievable. His aerobic capacity is such that he can repeat a great effort within seconds. His peripheral vision is such that if someone has his pocket picked in the stands during a game, Pele will probably know about it."

Pele seemed to be all over the field, often reaching a critical spot just before the action did. Not only did he know where to be, he was perpetually poised to spring like a cat in any direction. When the ball came near, Pele became a blur of forces all interacting like an eruption of gymnastic maneuvers. The result of such a flurry might be a perfect pass to a teammate for a clear shot at the goal, a breakaway dribble through the defense, or a sensational shot that had a goalie asking: "What happened?"

"I never realized a player could be aware of where everyone is on the field at a given moment," said Werner Roth, then captain of the Cosmos.

One of the greatest examples of Pele's talents occurred in the world club championship game in 1962 between Santos and the Portuguese squad. He scored three goals and passed for two others as Santos won, 5–2. On one of his scores he simply waited in front of the goal while two of his teammates passed the ball forward along the sideline and then shot it toward him. He was not alone, of course, for Pele was always double- and triple-teamed. As the ball came toward him and his defenders, Pele lifted his right leg in a short, quick motion and looped the ball over one de-

100

fenseman's head. He dodged past that man, lifted the ball again as two more defenders charged him. The ball seemed to hang in midflight as Pele feinted to his left. Then he ducked his shoulders and lunged between his opponents. Before a shocked goaltender could react, Pele had driven the ball into the net with his head.

A few years ago, medical experts examined Pele's compact, athletic figure for weeks in a university laboratory in Brazil. They prodded him, wired his head for readings, and measured his muscles and brain. When they finished they announced:

"Whatever this man might have decided to do in any physical or mental endeavor, he would have been a genius."

Physically, they said, Pele's feet are absolutely parallel, and his heels are so strong that they serve as a shock absorber after a jump. That could explain why Pele excelled at all aspects of soccer, while most other players were only adept at one or two. On defense, for example, Pele was a master at pilfering an opponent's dribble. On offense, his passing was unmatched, since with a flick of a heel, shoulder, or forehead, he could send the ball to the precise spot in the air or on the grass where a teammate could press the attack with the most potential for success.

Pele consistently outjumped taller rivals, and at the peak of his leap, after a head fake or two to get the goalie off balance, he could deftly nod the ball into a corner of the goal as unerringly as a slingshot.

A fast runner, Pele could sprint at top speed while controlling the ball in front of him. To an observer, it looked as if Pele and the ball were connected by a rubber band. Then in perfect rhythm, he could stop dead in his tracks, still dribbling, and gently plop the ball over a defender's head. Like a magnet, he would then dart around his opponent and pick up the ball on his toes before it even touched the ground.

It was said that Pele constantly planned four or five moves ahead, compared to most soccer players who hope to foresee two or three. If you play chess, it would be like planning your moves two turns ahead while playing a Bobby Fischer, who had the next five moves figured out.

"Pele is the only player," claimed a teammate, "who can think twice in one second."

Wrote another observer after watching Pele play: "When he rushes through the offensive zone toward a goal, Pele captures the imagination in a way that only the most dramatic of athletes can. He exhibits complete mastery in all that he does. He can, for a moment, make all the patterns and tactics of a complex game seem unimportant.

"And because it's so comprehensive, Pele's got all the options. I mean, he's not the kind of player who decides how he's going to take the ball up the field when he gets it. He just sees what's going on, and then he knows what's available."

Believe it or not, it is not Pele's skill with a soccer ball that has made his name synonymous with superstar. Though one can measure physical gifts with those of others, the competitive drive that distinguishes him cannot be measured. In modern sports, where stars are overpaid and become egotistical, Pele has never shown himself to be anything but charming, gracious, and patient, especially with the young. That's the indelible image a Pele leaves.

"I would like to be remembered," he said, "as a person who showed the world that the simplicity of a man is still the most important quality. Through simplicity and sincerity, you can put all humankind together."

There are many names by which Pele will be remembered, too. In Brazil, his native country, they called him "Perola Negra" (Black Pearl); in France, it was "La Tulipe Noire" (The Black Tulip); in Chile, he was known as "El Peligro" (the Dangerous One); in Italy as "Il Re" (the King); and in Greece as "O Vasilias" (Excellent One). Even Pele, of course, had nothing to do with his real name, which is Edson Arantes do Nascimento.

"Pele has done more good than all the ambassadors of

the world put together," said the Brazilian ambassador to the United States. Charles de Gaulle of France made Pele a Knight of the Order of Merit. In the early 1970s, a civil war in Biafra was stopped for two days because both sides wanted to see Pele play. Once, Pope Paul VI said to Pele: "Don't be nervous, my son. I am more nervous than you because I have been wanting to meet Pele personally for a long time."

Money and fame haven't changed Pele. His face always seems to be decorated with a pleasant smile and his generosity is greatest with his most valuable possession—himself. He will sign autographs until his arm tires, pose ungrudgingly for pictures, and talk to strangers as if they were doing him a favor.

Shep Messing, who was the Cosmos' goalie when Pele played there, said: "The thing I admire the most about Pele is his sincerity, integrity, and dedication to the game. He never gives up, never coasts, and always tried harder than any rookie."

He could have complained, and because he is Pele, people would have listened. He could have demanded changes in his rigorous schedule. He could have written his own ticket for his salary. But that was not Pele's style. He said that a man who gets paid to play a game should be happy, so Pele acted happy, satisfied, grateful. He was modest, but not quite to the point where it would sound phony. He was not just that way in public, either. He behaved the same in private.

Carlos Alberta, one of his teammates on the Brazilian team, said: "If I need a soda, Pele gets it for me."

Though he has had years and years of uninterrupted success, Pele never really prepared himself for anything. He greeted each new triumph with wide, appreciative eyes and the happy naiveté that was a mark of his style.

"Only God can explain all this," Pele said. "No smoking, no drinking, a clean life, maybe those are some of the reasons. When I was eleven, twelve years old, the other boys would say, 'Why don't you play for us?' and that is how I found I was any good."

In the United States most youngsters have no trouble getting their parents to buy them a baseball glove. Pele, born in poverty, had to earn his most cherished wish, a soccer ball. Constantly cutting school to earn money, he collected peanuts that had fallen off railroad cars, roasted them, then sold them to rich people.

His mother dreamed that he would grow up and become a professional man, perhaps a doctor, and earn a reliable living. "Football was the only career I ever thought of," Pele said, "though I became a cobbler's apprentice. I never really thought I'd stick to it. I wanted to follow my father's path as a football player because I was convinced he was the best player who ever lived but who never got a chance to prove it."

So as a boy, Pele was encouraged in his love of football, or soccer, as we call it here, by his father, Dondinho. He made Pele a soccer ball out of rags, and the youngster was often seen dribbling the ragged ball down the streets.

He would happily spend his time trying to juggle any handy soccer ball substitute, such as a grapefruit, with his foot, knee, shoulder, or head. About this time, his playmates started calling him "Pele," which is apparently just a nonsense term. He let them know that he didn't like the new nickname, so, naturally, it stuck.

By the time he was ten, soccer had taken such a strong hold on him that he dropped out of school after the fourth grade. Today, Pele calls his affinity for the game "destiny," adding: "I was born for soccer, just as Beethoven was born for music."

He continued to be tutored by his father until one day he was playing against men much older than he in a pickup game at a construction site. One of the men, Waldemir de Brito, was a former Santos player and a scout for Brazil's leading club. De Brito took him under his wing. For the next four years he taught Pele everything about soccer, and when the boy turned fifteen, he brought him to the Santos club for a tryout. He said to the Santos officials: "This boy will be the greatest player in the world."

He was signed to a contract for about $75 a month, and in his first game, he scored 4 goals. The legend was born. He scored 66 goals in that first year. Two years later, his body filled out, he scored 127 goals, his all-time high.

That year, in a hard-fought contest against a club from Sao Paolo, Pele played only a mediocre first half, and the fans razzed him unmercifully. But in the second half, he made a dazzling play for a goal and leaped exuberantly into the air, punching the sky with his fist.

"When I scored that goal," he said, "I felt some kind of explosion of my emotions. All the stress was gone, and I was feeling really free."

That "goal salute" became Pele's trademark, one that he repeated hundreds of times throughout his career. He had ninety-three 3-goal performances before he retired, and thirty-one 4-goal games. Six times he scored 5 goals in a game, while once he tallied 8 times in a single contest.

As Pele's records rose, both Santos and Brazil became dominant forces in the world of soccer. Amid rumors that Italian clubs were offering $1 million for Pele when he was just twenty, Brazil officially declared him a "national treasure," an asset that could not be exported.

Eventually, Pele made four times as much money as the president of his country, leading Brazil to three world championships. The event is held only once every four years.

After each World Cup victory, his Santos coach would be asked: "Is Pele the greatest player you've ever coached?" The coach would pause for effect and then say: "Pele is the greatest player anyone has ever coached."

Now a millionaire, Pele began to experience the problems of millionaire superstars. He would invariably be roughed up in crucial games, sometimes badly enough to send him to the hospital. Often he would come out and play despite the injuries.

So immensely popular, Pele would have to be surrounded by bodyguards in order not to be crushed by adoring fans wherever he went. Nevertheless, he would say: "I adore the crowds around me, especially the kids. I know that when I was growing up, football was one of the few things I could enjoy. Seeing a top player was always a big thrill. Now I get a thrill myself by having the kids around me. Of course, sometimes the people can get too enthusiastic."

The adoring mobs were the mark of Pele's supremacy. Every poll taken since 1958 declared him the world's premier soccer player.

The brutality directed against Pele grew on the soccer field, however. He called it "the consequences of my fame." In one World Cup match, the Bulgarian team worked him over, finally crippling him and costing the Brazilians whatever chance they had to win the cup again.

No matter what team he now played against, there was a man assigned just to guard him, to employ any method he could to stop him, legal or illegal. "There's always somebody gunning for me," Pele said. "I know that players are ordered to do it, and I don't hold it against them so much. They have to do their jobs. I've been pushed, tripped, kicked—every foul there is. If I tried the same thing against them, I'd be thrown out of the game. What makes me most angry is that the public pays to see me play good football, and then the other teams won't let me."

Responsibility has always been a Pele theme. Responsibility to his teammates, to the people who pay him and to his trusting fans. Responsibility to the thousands of kids who read Pele magazines, eat Pele candy bars, and do not smoke Pele cigarettes. He refuses to endorse any alcohol or tobacco products, and on one tour he turned down a $10,000 offer for one beer ad.

"It costs to give up such things," he said, "but it's one thing I can do to help the kids live good lives."

What is Pele's advice for youngsters who yearn to become sports heroes? "First, I would say, study with all your heart to become not just a star but a true sportsman.

"Second, it is important to be an intelligent listener and to follow advice from older players and your coach.

"Third, you must love what you are doing."

An appreciation of the model of this advice must be passed down secondhand now. In Brazil, parents tell their babies: "Too bad. You will not see Pele play."

Until 1975, Americans were told the same thing by soccer-loving fans. "You haven't seen anything," they would say, "till you've seen Pele." But that was beginning to look impossible, since Pele was already in retirement in Brazil.

Then the impossible happened. The only thing that could have brought Pele back into uniform again, the only challenge left in the world of soccer: to popularize the world's most popular sport among Americans, who seemed happily caught up in baseball, football, basketball, and hockey.

Said Pele, arriving in the U.S.: "I came to your country because I realized I was the only one who could help soccer here. Spread the news that soccer has finally arrived in the U.S."

Given soccer's lowly status here, nobody quite expected the mob scene that occurred when the New York Cosmos unveiled their prize specimen. Not counting the 300 newsmen, photographers, and hangers-on, a crowd of 20,124, double the usual turnout, cheered Pele. He wasn't even going to play. He was in street clothes.

When Pele joined the Cosmos, they were a ragtag collection playing their home games in dingy Downing Stadium on Randalls Island in New York's East River. One newsman summed up Pele's appearance there as "comparable to putting the Mona Lisa on display in a Hoboken body shop." Another said after watching Pele attempt to direct his awed teammates into effective playing patterns: "It was like Toscanini trying to coax a moving performance out of a junior-high-school band."

But when the team finally moved into Yankee Stadium and visited such indigenously American cities as Seattle, Tampa, and Indianapolis, the crowds grew tremendously. A crowd of 28,000 turned up for the opener in New York. In Seattle, 58,128 fans showed up, the largest soccer crowd in U.S. history. The next year, at Giants Stadium in New Jersey, a record 76,000 spectators jammed their way in.

As the Cosmos' general manager put it: "U.S. soccer went from the Stone Age to the Jet Age in one jump with Pele's arrival."

Added the Cosmos' captain: "There is no way we would have drawn 76,000 without Pele, the most sincere, helpful, and dedicated man that I have seen. The guy is unbelievable."

Finally, it came down to Pele's emotionally charged farewell appearance on October 1, 1977, at Giants Stadium. At the heart of Pele's game is always a joyful pursuit of the impossible. He had dominated the mythology of soccer as no man had before him. He had scored more goals as a professional than anyone else. He had created thousands of moments of exhilarating beauty. Yet, he had never hidden the insistent desire to do the impossible, to score the goal that would stand apart from all the others, the goal that no one could emulate: the Pele goal.

In his final moment, then, in his 1,363rd game as a professional, Pele scored his 1,281st goal. It was the goal that tied the game, and it will never be emulated. The Cosmos were awarded a free kick thirty yards from the goal, and Pele took it with blistering force. Before anyone could say "Pele," the ball was off the inside of his right foot and into the net. The noise from the crowd could be heard in Brazil. Pele had done the impossible again.

Franz Beckenbauer, his teammate and a player whom many consider will be Pele's successor, added the final tribute. "Pele is the most perfect man I know. I could never hope to be his equal."

# 9

# PHIL ESPOSITO

## Born to Score

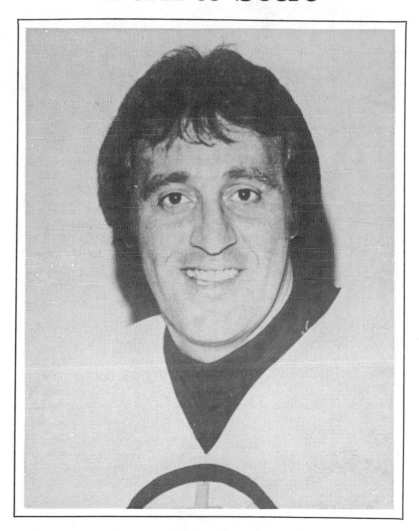

What is a hockey superstar? A whirlwind who can skate faster than anybody else? A sleight-of-hand stick-handler who can keep the puck away from the other team? A clairvoyant who instinctively seems to know where the puck is going to be? A strongarm shooter who can fire the puck over a hundred miles an hour?

Yes, all of these attributes can qualify a hockey player for stardom. But did we forget something? You still have to put the puck in the net. You still have to beat out the defender, the poke-checker, the body-checker, and the goalie. They still pay off on just one thing: the score.

Goals are the name of the game, and nowhere has there been a goal-scorer more prolific than Phil Esposito. The National Hockey League center won't pick up laurels for speed, nor does he remind anyone of an Olympic figure-skater. His shot does not bowl you over, either, but when you check the record book, you'll see that Esposito has been turning the red light on at a faster pace than anybody else.

Records? When Esposito started breaking records, he didn't just break them—he shattered them. When Esposito set his first record for most points, it was 29 points higher than history's previous best mark.

Only one player had ever scored more than 50 goals until Esposito set his mind to that task. Bobby Hull had once scored 58, but Esposito got 76 in a season to bury that figure. And to prove it was no fluke, the next season he totaled 66 goals, then 56, then 68, and then 61.

How does he do it? "It's simple," Esposito says. "First off: If you don't shoot, you don't score."

An opponent paid him the ultimate compliment one day by saying: "When you play against Espo, you start at least one goal down."

Another added: "Esposito combines reach, strength, intelligence, and competitiveness to such a degree that the only way he can be countered is with superbly coordinated defensive play. Still, even that might not be enough."

111

Of course, it's a lot more than just shooting. Many players with good shots never get more than two or three chances a game. Esposito usually finds a dozen opportunities.

"There's more to it than that," he admits. "For one thing, I stopped aiming—a long time ago. Bobby Hull told me once that the more time you take to aim at a spot, the more chance there is the goalie will be there first. True, there are times when you have a split-second to aim, but in the vast majority of cases I simply let it go when I'm milling around the net.."

"Milling around the net," Esposito calls it. The slot, most other players say, referring to the area about fifteen feet in front of the net between the two face-off circles. It's the "sweet spot" of hockey, where you'd like to be most of all if you want to score, and the place where more muggings take place, legally and illegally, than anywhere else in a hockey rink.

Anyone who dares take up a stance in the slot for more than a second usually finds the butts of defensemen's sticks rapping him in the stomach. If that fails to budge him, the elbows begin to fly, with the ribs, neck, and head as primary targets. Sticks lash at the ankles, gloves dart out to puncture the nose, and, finally, karate-style defenders will throw themselves on top of the human invader until they all go down in a heap. It is impossible to score lying stretched out on the ice with two or three bodies lying on you.

Esposito's secret lies in being able to weather this kind of treatment long enough to get the puck and send it winging into the cage. The slot, he feels, is his home and where he belongs if he wants to help his team score goals. No one else in the N.H.L. can perform that function as well as Esposito.

"He stays in there so long we should be able to move him out some way," said a Toronto defenseman. "But sometimes he doesn't even budge when he gets hit."

112

Esposito tolerates most of this punishment for three main reasons: one, maybe he will receive a pass from one of his wingers, whereupon he will shoot at almost the same instant the puck is on his stick; two, he may be able to tip in a shot from one of his defensemen firing away from the blue line; three, he may find a juicy rebound from a teammate's shot. "Garbage goals"—that's what those rebounds around the cage are called. And "super garbage collector" is what a lot of envious folk call Esposito's talent in that respect. It may not sound nice, but ask a team that owns one.

Esposito's opponents don't step aside, however, when a rebound lands on Phil's stick. He may not own the booming slapshot of a Bobby Hull, his teammate for many years on the Chicago Black Hawks, nor the cleverness of Montreal's Guy Lafleur. But Esposito has to have something else that allows him to collect all that garbage. What he has is a deceptively quick and deadly accurate wrist drive.

"I'm not spectacular like a Bobby Orr or a Guy Lafleur," Espo says. "I know it and I admit it. But I also know that my role is to score goals, to pick up loose pucks and put them behind the goaltender any way I can. So that's what I try to do—and people still call me a garbage collector."

Why doesn't every center stand in the slot and wait for the puck and score lots of goals? The answer is, they can't, at least not like Esposito, who offers very special considerations to his very special role: size, strength, skill.

First, size. Esposito cannot easily be missed in a hockey rink; he's 6 feet 1 inch and 210 pounds. In his heyday he was the most massive player in the league. He takes that hulk and, like a tree, he plants it in front of the opposing goalie. Not too close, however. He is not permitted inside the crease, the rectangular area, 6 feet by 4 feet, in front of the cage.

So it happens like this: When Esposito's team corrals the puck, Esposito sets sail for the slot. But he doesn't just stand there. He parks his huge frame in that dangerous

113

area and sets up housekeeping. Said Bobby Orr: "Phil must rent the slot from the Garden." Now, everybody on his team is either trying to get open for a good shot or get the puck to Esposito. Owner of one of hockey's quickest sticks, he fires away with slingshot ease.

"He gets the puck and bangs it into the goal while you're still trying to figure out how he got the puck in the first place," say his frustrated rivals. "And he's strong enough to fend off a defenseman with one arm and skate right around him. The only way I know to stop him is to put somebody on him and shadow him constantly. In the end, though, that just opens things up for his linemates. And they usually score."

Though 6 feet 1 and 210 doesn't sound that big for a professional athlete, by hockey standards, it is very large. The average N.H.L. player is a shade under 6 feet and weighs 187 pounds. The difference was even more marked at the start of Espo's career when players were a lot smaller than they are today.

"Because I'm big," he says, "it makes it harder for defensemen to push me out of the way. But I also have a long and heavy stick—it's 4 ounces heavier than the normal stick and it must weigh 23 ounces. It's also the longest stick allowed, 55 inches. The blade is 3 inches wide, which is also the widest you're permitted.

"So if a defenseman plays my body, he still can't get around me to tie up my arms because they're so long. And, at the end, I have my stick, which is long. So the defenseman has to get past me to get to the stick, and he can't do that, usually."

Sometimes, though, in frustration or anger, defensemen will resort to stopping Esposito with methods that are far from legal. In Central Park it's called mugging, but on the ice, a lot happens when the referee isn't looking that isn't written in the rules.

"I don't think I should be granted immunity or anything," Esposito says, "but I believe referees should watch for infractions more closely in the slot. Let's face it, I get fouled more than most players, but refs don't seem to pay much attention to that fact. If something happens, they say I should expect it because I'm a star."

When he was with Boston, Esposito had teammates nearly as big as he—Ken Hodge and Wayne Cashman. Altogether, they weighed more than 600 pounds and stood over 18 feet in height. The Esposito-Hodge-Cashman line set a single-season scoring record of 336 points in 1970–71. While Espo was clogging up the middle, Hodge and Cashman were throwing their weight around in the corners, coming up with the puck and sending it special-delivery to their almost automatic goal-scorer.

"We went at them in waves," Esposito recollected, "and it didn't hurt to have an Orr firing those cannon shots of his from the point."

Thus loaded, Esposito went on to become the N.H.L.'s second all-time leading scorer—and a good bet to become No. 1 before he retires—as well as a setter of hockey's most prized offensive records. Some of them include: most hat-tricks (32); most consecutive 40-or-more-goal seasons (seven); most consecutive 50-or-more-goal seasons (five); most 100-or-more-point seasons (six); most goals in a season (76); most points one season (152); most points in one playoff year (27), and most power-play goals one season (28).

What many fans forget, though, is that Phil Esposito broke into the league with the reputation as a feeder, not a scorer, and he carried that responsibility for the four seasons he played with the Black Hawks. There was a good reason: Bobby Hull, another prolific goal-scorer, was also a Black Hawk. During those years, Esposito never scored more than 27 goals or more than 61 points in any season. But the first year he was traded to Boston, in 1967–68, he led the league in assists. He became an All-Star and has been one ever since.

"When Phil went to Boston, he changed his style," said Nick Garen, the Rangers' trainer, who was the Black

Hawks' trainer in those days. "When he was in Chicago, he would rather pass the puck to Bobby, who was going for the record, 58. Phil was his center when he scored the 58th."

Hull, who retired from pro hockey in 1978 but returned last season, is still a close friend of Espo's, and he still likes to rave about his old teammate. What Hull likes to point out is that for two seasons after they traded Esposito, the Hawks slumped and missed the playoffs.

On the other hand, the year Esposito joined the Bruins, their fortunes changed. "We were a last-place team," said Orr. "Then with Esposito, we won the championship—twice. The minute Phil came to Boston, the whole team changed. Give the credit to Esposito."

Not only did Esposito produce the scoring punch so badly needed, Orr explained, but he also brought the team together spiritually. He'd say, "C'mon, guys, I know we can make the playoffs, but we got to stick together." Orr added that Esposito was even more important off the ice.

While Esposito has proved himself a serious taskmaster on the ice, a leader and happy-go-lucky guy off the ice, not many people realize the long struggle it took to reach the heights. It really began in childhood when Phil and his brother Tony (a goaltender with the Black Hawks) competed in a tabletop hockey game, Phil shooting the marble like mad and Tony making save after save.

When their father refinished the basement into a long recreation room, the brothers strapped pads on their knees and began playing kneeling indoor hockey, slapping a rolled-up woolen sock up and down the "ice" with their hands. When they were a little bit older, they took their act to the rink. "We used to get up at four-thirty or five in the morning," Phil said, "load Tony's goal pads and everything on the toboggan and pull it right through town to the rink so we could practice before school.

"Usually I did the shooting and Tony the goaltending. It's like baseball; every kid wants to get up and take his swings, and every Canadian kid wants to shoot the puck. I was a year older, so I did the shooting. Maybe Tony didn't like it, but he didn't have much choice."

Phil played his first pro hockey when he was barely twenty. He played for the Soo Thunderbirds in his hometown, but when the parent club, the Black Hawks, came to take a look at Esposito, he was wearing a cast on his left wrist. Don't ask Espo how that happened, but the truth is, when he tried to leave the penalty box too fast, he fell headlong on the ice and broke a bone in his wrist.

Nevertheless, despite the cast, Esposito picked up three assists in front of a Hawk scout and was invited to the Chicago camp, where he won a contract. He started slowly but gradually fitted into the system that had him feeding Hull.

Esposito, as big as he is, was never particularly muscular. ("I've got long muscles," he says, half kiddingly, "long and concealed. Why, I measured 36–36–36 when I was fourteen years old.")

Garen, the trainer, says Espo's skin is soft, too. But all this doesn't mean he isn't strong. "In front of the net," says Garen, "Espo is like a balanced tripod. He's very powerful in the arms and legs. Now, take Bobby Hull, who has a wonderful upper torso, very muscular. But you never see Bobby Hull in front of the net. His legs aren't so well-developed and he can be knocked down."

Everyone notices Phil's size first of all, and many let it go at that: he's so big, that's why he scores so often. But there are at least three other factors that account for Espo's consistency: He is smart. He knows hockey theory and how to practice to achieve the desired results. In fact, when he isn't playing, he runs hockey schools during the off-season. That's one reason he could shift so easily from a playmaker to a scorer. With the New York Rangers, he carries the puck more than he did with the Bruins. He can do both jobs. And he is expected to become the Ranger coach when his playing days are over.

Stemming from this intelligence are the technical attributes that keep him among the league leaders. One of these is the fact that he keeps his stick on the ice—constantly. Watch a hockey game and you notice that some players skate with their sticks in the air. Esposito's stick is always on the ice. If the puck happens to wind up near him, the shot is released with no wasted motion.

One more thing: Where most forwards come off the ice to rest after ninety seconds or so, Esposito often is double-shifted for up to three minutes at a stretch, and the reasons for that are obvious: The more you play, the more chances you get to shoot. The more you shoot, the more goals you score, especially if you're Phil Esposito.

"Esposito is really underrated because he's not a spectacular scorer," says Ken Dryden, the former Montreal Canadiens' goaltender. "He doesn't have the slither shot or the big booming shot, but he scores goals better than anybody. He wears you down. He gets nine or ten shots a game, and he gets about a goal a game. That may not be a very high percentage, but over a season, it adds up. He simply bombards you."

Two players have taken more than 400 shots in a season. Hull took 414 in the 1968–69 campaign when he got his 58 goals. But Esposito broke the shooting record by 136 shots when he scored his 76 goals in 1970–71.

To Dryden, who had the best spot in the house to watch, Esposito excels because "he controls his stick better than anybody, deflects the puck better than anybody, which requires a lot of eye-hand coordination, and he is bigger than nearly anybody else."

Dryden added: "The best thing a goalie has going for him when it comes to Esposito is that, on a pass from the corner to the center, you know he's going to shoot it quickly. So you're set. With anyone else, you might relax. With Espo, you know he'll get his stick on the puck somehow, and he does.

"That's his game. Of the eight, nine, or ten shots a game on net from him, very few are setup efforts in which

118

he picks his spot. Most are passes that he shoots immediately—the quickness of release and shortness of shot cause the problem.

"There's nobody else in hockey over the last seven or eight years that makes you automatically know there's a goal on the board before a game begins. Nobody approximates that kind of success."

The measure of a superstar's greatness is most evident in a high-pressure situation that can match the peak of a player's skill. The N.H.L. provides that kind of confrontation over a long, extended period, but the highest provocation for championship spirits to flare and ignite people's imaginations needs a short, ultra-important series. This was more than sufficient in the first historic meeting of the Canadian hockey stars and the Soviet Union's best in September 1972.

That year, the two hockey powers agreed to play eight games to decide the world's superiority in the sport. No holds barred, anybody can play, no excuses later. Team Canada, comprising most of the N.H.L.'s top players, was as confident of victory over the upstart Russians as could be.

Phil Esposito, the champion scorer of the N.H.L. for the third straight season, naturally was a part of that Canadian team. And, as was his wont, he led the charge. He scored the first goal after only thirty seconds of the first game. He scored the first goal of the second game and assisted on another. In the third game, he assisted on the first goal and scored the third goal. In the fourth game, he assisted on two goals. And in the seventh game, he scored the opening goal and the second goal.

With such a record, you'd think the Canadians would have held a 7–0 lead in games, wouldn't you? Not so, even though those first seven games were played in Canada. Russia won the opener, 7–3, shocking the world. Canada came back to take the second, 4–1, and the teams tied in the third, 4–4.

But Canada lost the fourth game, 5–3, and then split the next two. In the seventh contest, Espo again scored the opening goal and followed it up with a goal that tied the score before Canada came on to win, 4–3.

Thus, the stage was set—before an astonished hockey world: Each team had won three games and lost three, with one tie. The climactic eighth game was to be played in Moscow.

By now the Russians knew all about Esposito, and for the finale, they were ordered to double-team the big Canadian scorer. The supremacy of hockey was up for grabs!

In less than four minutes, the Russians took a 1–0 lead and their fans roared with approval. But at the seven-minute mark, Canada tied the score on a goal by—Esposito. That was the fourth time in eight games he had scored his team's first goal.

In the second period, the Russians kept to their slick passing and skating game and ran up a 5–3 lead over Canada. They were looking to supply the crusher when along came—our man, Espo. At 2:27 of the third period, Espo scored his second goal of the game to make it 5–4. Then at 12:56 he set up Yvan Cournoyer with a perfect feed, and the resulting goal made it 5–5.

A minute and a half later, a Soviet skater outraced the Canadian defense and came in alone on Dryden in goal. He deked Dryden out of the crease, swept the puck away from the outreached glove of the sprawling goaltender and sent it toward the empty net. Out of nowhere came a stick to deflect the puck to the boards. Whose stick? Esposito's.

The score remained tied till the last minute of the game. Then, with just 34 seconds left on the clock, a pileup occurred in front of the Russian net. Out of the pile came Esposito with the puck. He sent it to his teammate, Paul Henderson, who fired it into the net. Canada had won the game and the series—thanks mainly to Esposito.

"That series," said a columnist in a Canadian newspaper, "would not have been won without Esposito's big, rough, relentless leadership. I saw him make what will become a hockey heirloom passed down through the generations."

Esposito is thirty-eight years old now and winding down a marvelous career. Five times an Art Ross Trophy winner as the league's leading scorer, Espo still trails Gordie Howe as the league's all-time best point-scorer and goal scorer. But he is considered the only one capable of catching Howe and breaking those marks. He's got 710 goals, and they're still counting.

# 10
# TOM SEAVER
## Total Concentration

Talk about great baseball pitchers and you think of great arms. Continuing that thought process, you think of the raw power great arms can generate, whipping around sideways like a Ewell Blackwell, cracking out of nowhere like a Don Drysdale, blazing a fastball with a high hop like a Bob Gibson, or snapping off a brutal drop like a Sandy Koufax.

You also think of the other physical assets of the better pitchers, the strong legs of a Walter Johnson, the massive torso of Don Newcombe, the wide shoulders of a Bob Feller, or the crooked elbow of a Carl Hubbell.

Not many of us will consider the intelligence of a pitcher when greatness is mentioned, at least not at first. We forget how inevitably the very good batters will catch up to the rhythm of the very good pitchers who rely on power and physique alone.

It's the brainy hurlers, however, who combine a mental acuity with God-given power who produce a combination devoutly desired by any major-league manager. The outstanding example of such a pitcher is Tom Seaver, who has devoted his athletic life toward perfecting the art of pitching as if it were a science. In doing so he became baseball's No. 1 practitioner of imparting a high degree of intellect into a flashing right arm, two powerful legs, and a strong body.

The results of this amalgam seem to prove that this is the ultimate secret of becoming a superstar on the mound. At least, Seaver's scientific approach to the game of baseball made him the greatest pitcher for a full decade.

Seaver won the Cy Young Award as the best pitcher in the National League three times. He set a major-league record by striking out 200 or more batters for nine consecutive seasons. (In another year, 1977, he recorded 196 to miss by four of making it ten.) His lifetime earned-run average of 2.55 is second only to Walter Johnson's 2.47 among pitchers who have won at least 200 major-league games. And Seaver's career winning percentage of .639

(235 victories, 133 defeats) is second only to Whitey Ford's .690 among pitchers who have worked in the major leagues since 1945. What you should bear in mind, of course, is that Seaver accomplished most of this while with the New York Mets, a club whose down years far outnumber its up years.

"I'm happiest when I'm pitching," Seaver has admitted, even to his wife, Nancy. "That's what motivates me. There are some pitchers who want to go down in history as the fastest pitcher. Others want to win 30 games in a season. And there are those who think pitching a no-hitter is the end-all of the sport, or maybe winning a World Series game. But all I want to do is the best I can—day after day, year after year. Maybe that will someday make me the best ever."

To take the first step in becoming baseball's best pitcher, you have to get the batters out, and Seaver has done that with frightening regularity. Averaging about thirty-five to forty starting assignments per season for the Mets and later the Cincinnati Reds, he has allowed less than 2.5 earned runs for every nine innings he pitched. which means, of course, that if the Mets or Reds scored just 3 or 4 runs a game, he—and they—would have outstanding seasons.

From 1967, when he first joined the Mets, till the beginning of the 1980 season with the Reds, that represents 3,454 innings. It also includes 235 victories, 2,887 men struck out, five one-hitters and a no-hit game. No wonder New Yorkers called him "The Franchise."

When he hurled his 48th shutout, he became the leader in that department, too, among active pitchers.

"Pitching is a continual learning process," Seaver will tell you. (He's been saying that since he first joined the majors.) "I feel that I know how to pitch, yet I'm learning more about how to pitch all the time. That's why I feel pitching is a creative art and why I find it stimulating."

Until that day comes when Seaver says he's learned all

there is to pitching, he will continue to follow a "total" rationale, leaving little to chance. How does he come to formulate this rationale?

"The initial thing is to formulate the theory that you're going to work under. Mine is to strive for consistency, and there are four elements to it: mental preparation, physical preparation, the mechanics of pitching, and game strategy."

This then is Seaver's—or any pitcher's—problem: To toss, with some finesse and speed, a cowhide sphere weighing between 5 ounces and 5¼ ounces a distance of 60½ feet toward a home plate that is 12 inches across and 17 inches deep and that is guarded by a man swinging a 33-ounce or heavier wooden bat.

These are Seaver's credentials for achieving the above: Age: 35; weight: 200 pounds; height: 6 feet 1 inch; education: graduate of the University of Southern California; experience: one season in the minors (Jacksonville, where he won 12 and lost 12, with a 3.13 e.r.a., in 1966); 14 seasons in the majors.

He's older than Nolan Ryan, who throws harder. He's shorter than Jim Palmer, who has better control. He weighs less than Mickey Lolich, a better fielder. He's less gregarious than Luis Tiant, who's more imaginative on the mound. He's less clinical than Mike Marshall, who possesses more pitches. And he's less unruffled than Catfish Hunter, who made more money. But to most observers, Seaver has shown more effectiveness at getting people out than any of the other 240 active pitchers in baseball.

"Some athletes bring tremendous physical strength into it," Seaver said. "O. J. Simpson starts with more physical ability in football than I do in baseball. Willie Mays starts with more in baseball than I do. Willie McCovey starts with more size and strength than the rest of us.

"So to match that kind of talent, I have to hoard my energies, sometimes at the expense of other activities in my life. Therefore, when it comes to baseball, my theory is to strive for consistency and not worry about the 'numbers.' If you dwell on stats, you get short-sighted. If you aim for consistency, the numbers will be there at the end, believe me. My job isn't to go out and strike guys out. It's to get them out, and sometimes you get them out by striking them out."

What brings such tremendous consistency? You're not born with it; you make it, as Seaver does, by great attention to detail, fierce concentration, and an unremitting willpower. Here's an example: One night Seaver and his teammates returned from a road trip at about 10 P.M. The exhausted players could only think of one thing, getting home and relaxing. Not Tom. He took a cab from the airport to Shea Stadium, which at that hour was dark, deserted, and damp.

He went to his locker, changed into his uniform and went out to the bullpen carrying a bag of baseballs. Then he took the mound and fired baseball after baseball into the bullpen screen. When his supply of balls was exhausted, he walked to the screen, picked them all up, and then threw them again. This went on for twenty minutes, Seaver throwing baseballs into the screen in an empty ballpark in the dead of night. Later, someone asked him why he did that. Seaver answered: "It was my day to throw. I always throw on my day to throw."

That's typical Seaver-ana. And to Tom, actions speak as loud as his words, which are as perfectionistic as his deeds. One of the most analytical athletes, Seaver sometimes sounds like a professional consultant hired to study himself. While some players offer vague reasons for their success, or how they operate under pressure, Seaver comes on with a complete text. He not only has a fully prepared program of facts, but he also includes a great stage presence.

"The No. 1 significant thing for me," he says, "is mental. I mean by that an awareness of yourself and what you can or can't do. About five years ago, I started to understand it all, that pitching is not just throwing a baseball. I began to understand why the right leg has to drive and why the left arm has to wheel so that your shoulders achieve momentum and speed.

"No. 2 for me," he continued, "is physical. You have to control all the physical aspects that influence your performance, like sleep and diet. They add up to self-discipline. Who decides my diet? I do. I'll choose steak rather than spaghetti, even if a scientist says to forget it because there's no difference between steak and spaghetti. Even if it has no effect on my body chemically, it has a tremendous effect psychologically."

If Seaver has an idol, it might be Jack Nicklaus, who practices the mental and physical approach to golf the way Seaver would like to for baseball. When Seaver watches Jack play golf, he can see the enormous mental ability Nicklaus is putting into his effort. "I think that because my father was a golfer," explains Seaver, "it definitely gave me a sense of competition and discipline. And that's become the key to everything I do."

Pitching in the big leagues is not one big rosy joy ride no matter how good a pitcher you might be. There are days you just don't feel "right," when maybe your biorhythms are out of sync with the manager's orders for you to pitch. There are days when you feel great, but even so, the batters hit nearly everything you throw up there anyway. You can't figure it out. There are days you are sick, sore-armed, and, worst of all, injured. These are the times when the discipline Seaver talks about can save your career.

In 1974 Seaver was afflicted with a sore hip. He pitched through the year anyway—suffered through the summer, you might say—because it turned out to be his worst ever: 11 victories, 11 defeats, and allowing one more earned run every game than he had done in the past. One run, that was all, but it proved the critical difference between winning and losing.

Once Seaver traced the source of his injury to a spasmatic sciatic nerve that pained him as he delivered the ball and made him alter his pitch slightly, he knew what he had to do. Return to the basics and correct the mistakes. So thoroughly did he overcome that disabling malady that he came back the next season to win 22 games, strike out 243 batters, and earn his third Cy Young Award. Another pitcher might have faded into obscurity.

"The big thing with knowing yourself in a physical sense," he says, "is understanding what you need. My brother Charles is a sculptor and artist in Massachusetts, and through him I began to do stretching exercises. He does an hour and a half of yoga every day, so I decided to start yoga exercises to stretch my muscles.

"I was never very strong when I was young, at least not a big, strong high school athlete like the bonus kind. But the strongest part of my body was my legs. The older you get, the more you need to rely on the strength and suppleness of those legs, especially if your career is in baseball. So to keep them fit, I exercise for twenty minutes every day. A pitcher should never forget that driving off your legs is super-important for pitching. It takes the pressure off your shoulders and elbow."

Every pitcher hits a slump sometime or other, and Seaver was no different in that respect. But it took all the intellectual force he possessed not to let it get him down permanently. The injury would heal, but the psyche needed special attention. Seaver can look back on that slump and remember. Was it just the hip injury? Or was it his age (thirty) catching up to him and taking something off his torrid fastball? Was he reaching the end of a brilliant career as all pitchers must?

"Every pitcher goes through a phase, a transition period where he suffers," Seaver said. "You realize it, but the important thing is to adjust to it. You can't let it shoot down your career. Anyone with intelligence has got to realize it can happen in every professional sport. So it entered my mind: Either I pitch effectively or I don't have a job. It was as simple and as frustrating as that."

Some people thought that Seaver's problem that year stemmed from the fact that he was a "power pitcher" in an era of power hitting. He must challenge every hitter because, simply to him, it is always a question of excellence, the one goal he craves. So he became intense, with the result that nearly each of the 100 or more pitches he throws in a game is a crucial, money pitch.

At the time, Seaver said: "All my career I've been able to deal with pitching problems because I know how to go about it. First I have to be aware that I have a problem. Then I have to define what it is. And, finally, I have to solve it."

Until he ultimately solved the biggest problem he had ever faced, Seaver said he suffered emotional strain. "When I couldn't throw the ball hard, I tried to throw it harder. That only served to confuse me, and it wasn't long before I hit the low point emotionally."

Seaver's total commitment to his first love, pitching, brought him back to the peak of his profession. "I've devoted my life to this," he says, "and I should know what to do when something's not working."

When he's not pitching, Seaver is thinking pitching. "I live my life around the four or five days between starts," he notes. "It determines what I eat, when I go to bed, what I do when I'm awake. If it means I have to remind myself to pet dogs with my left hand, then I do it. If it means in the winter I eat cottage cheese instead of chocolate-chip cookies to keep my weight down, then I eat cottage cheese. I enjoy that cottage cheese more than I would those cookies because it'll help me do what makes me happy."

The attention to detail occurs even more so on the mound. Once he has warmed up, stridden out to the 24-inch-long rubber slab, planted his foot, looked down at the catcher for the sign, and checked the batter, it boils down to two final factors: the mechanics of hurling the ball and the strategy of hurling it in a sequence of pitches that will neutralize the batter's strength.

"I've varied the height of my leg in kicking and the length of my stride in stepping toward the plate," said Seaver, "but I never get too deeply immersed in the geometry of it, the height of the mound, or the distance to the plate. I'm more concerned with the conditions that prevail that day—the wind, the type of surface on the field, and the batters I'll be facing.

"You can't concentrate on the mechanics while you're pitching; it should be automatic. You're holding the ball in your right hand, you stretch out your left arm as you rotate your body clockwise toward second base, and then you wheel toward the plate to pitch the ball. That's when you must uncoil your left arm almost as though you're giving somebody a shot to the chest with it—driving off the mound with your legs and giving your shoulders the speed and momentum.

"I don't ever visualize myself in the act of pitching or the path of the ball. I do visualize the spot where I want the ball to end up."

Calling it a "guessing game" when a good pitcher meets a good batter, Seaver illustrated the following scenario of how he might pitch to Hank Aaron, the home-run king of baseball:

"Let's say the score is tied, and I don't want to give up a home run. Aaron, on the other hand, is looking for a pitch to hit out of the park. So the contest starts. Will I try to get him out on a ground ball or a fly ball, or what? It's a sequence of pitches I'm considering, and it may change on one pitch if it doesn't go right somewhere along the line. I'm not trying to get Aaron out on every pitch in the sequence, mostly I'm setting him up for the final pitch.

"I hold the ball loosely when I'm pitching, and you could probably reach in and pry it loose. But I can throw it fast, very fast, and I can intimidate batters if I have to. When you can move your fastball, nothing destroys a batter like a low fastball that rises into the strike zone.

"But a superbatter like Aaron is beyond that, so I have

to work on him. For the first pitch, I would throw a fastball or hard slider (which looks like a fastball coming to the plate but which breaks or slides away from him at the last moment). I'm trying for a strike, but I'm also trying to keep it away from his power because in most cases, Aaron will be looking for something inside to pull. This one breaks away, so he lays off. The umpire says strike one.

"On my second pitch, I throw a sinker that drops inside, but off the inside corner of the plate. I'm trying to get him to think this is the pitch he's looking for: inside, where he can yank it to left field. But I throw it too far inside for him to hit solidly and it drops anyway. Aaron fouls it off, let's say.

"Now he's seen both my fastball and my fast sinker, so for the third pitch I throw him a curve ball—away. He lays off again because it breaks outside away from his power. He takes it, hoping it's called a ball. It is, and now the count is 1 ball, 2 strikes.

"I'm still ahead on the count, so he can't be too choosy. Now I'll try to win the contest, but not on one pitch. I'll try a sequence of two pitches, starting with a curve and following with a slider—because I can afford to draw him out. In neither case, though, will I throw him a ball that he can pull out of the park. Aaron is a dead pull-hitter who might reach out and punch a single to right field, but not out of the park. Anyway: it's a curve ball, and he still might punch it to right (or he might take it for ball 2).

"If there is a need for a fifth pitch, it'll be the slider. If a sixth pitch is necessary, I might run the string out with a fastball upstairs—and hope he doesn't hit it upstairs."

Seaver has met the great hitters over and over, setting them down more often than they have set upon him. Until 1978, however, when he finally notched his first no-hit game, it was the little hitter who had been his bugaboo.

Three times, for instance, Seaver had gone to the ninth inning without having allowed a hit. And before he finally achieved his masterpiece, three times he came away empty-handed. His closest brush with a no-hitter came in 1975 against the Chicago Cubs. There were two outs and two strikes on Joe Wallis, but he singled. On July 9, 1969, he had a perfect game (nobody reaching base) with one out in the ninth, also against the Cubs. But Jimmy Qualls broke that up with a single. And he lost a no-hitter in the ninth inning on July 4, 1972, when Leron Lee of San Diego singled.

San Diego was just getting even for what Seaver had done to them in 1970 when he set a major league mark of 10 consecutive strikeouts against that club. He recorded 19 strikeouts for that contest, matching the major-league record for a nine-inning game.

"I'll tell you about Seaver," says Sparky Anderson, the former manager of the Reds. "For 250 innings, he's the best pitcher in baseball. These American League teams that face him in the series have never seen him at his best. Baseball is an endurance test. With all the night games and traveling around the country for 162 games, they all start to drag by August. It takes supreme stamina to last."

So Tom Terrific has that figured, too, and he hoards his energies. "I don't have the stamina and mental concentration to live the rest of my life with the same intensity I do baseball," he says. "I can't be a perfectionist in other things, too. In things other than baseball, I deliberately don't tap this competitiveness and concentration in me.

"Maybe I'm saving it for baseball. It must be like an energy source that has its limits. If I use it up on too many things, I'll have nothing left for baseball."

The record speaks for itself. Seaver became the best right-handed pitcher of his time because he concentrated on becoming the best. It is really as simple as that.

# 11

# JACK NICKLAUS

## Deadly Determination

What's perfection on a golf course? Par on every hole? Birdies? Eagles? Three-hundred-yard drives, irons dead to the pin, one-putt greens? Or is perfection constituted in monetary terms, winning a million dollars every year on the tour, capturing all the big-money tournaments, and keeping a caddy in the high-income bracket?

Maybe perfection to a golfer is winning when he has to, rising to the pressure of a 15-foot putt with the title on the line, going head to head with the best competition and finishing on top. Or it could be the ability to monitor power when necessary, accuracy when called for, delicacy at the proper moment, and absolute concentration when all about you bedlam reigns.

There is a golfer with these qualities. The man they're calling the greatest golfer the world has ever seen. Jack Nicklaus. But did you ever stop to realize how one person, using the same fourteen clubs everyone else uses, could reach the lofty status where people start comparing him to that unattainable goal: perfection?

What's Jack Nicklaus's secret that caused a fellow pro to mutter: "We're playing one game, and Jack Nicklaus is playing another."

In golf, it's impossible to single out one component of a man's game and term it entirely responsible. You have to be able to hit long, straight drives from the tees to set yourself up for the percentage shot to the green. Nicklaus is famed for that, but so are a number of other pros.

You have to be able to select the right iron, hold the green, and then putt surely and consistently. Nicklaus also does all that well, and so do others. You must possess the proper attitude to execute these shots when under the severest kind of pressure, which Nicklaus—and others—can do. And you've got to combine steely nerves, agile brainpower, and a good supply of muscle along with stamina to make all of the above work. Though Nicklaus shines in those departments, he is still not alone.

We haven't mentioned that element within an athlete

that lets him direct his thinking so intently that it closes out the rest of the world, so to speak. Deadly concentration, it's called. Jack Nicklaus is considered able to perform that trick as well as or better than any golfer who ever lived.

Several stories about Nicklaus's ability to concentrate have circulated through the golf fraternity. Here's one: A windy day at the Firestone Country Club in Akron, Ohio, has been giving the tour golfers fits. Besides blowing their drives off course and preventing them from estimating distances correctly, the gusty breezes are causing all kinds of noise. Spectators rustle about in the leaves, paper and debris blow across the golfers' vision, and things flap, destroying concentration.

As Nicklaus tees up his ball, a hanging sign that lists the yardage for that hole creaks loudly back and forth. A pure destroyer for golfers trying to collect their thoughts. Nearly every player has, upon addressing the ball, stepped back and glared at the sound, as if that would make it stop. The high squeak persists, however, proving worse than other golfers' peeves, such as camera clicks, loud whispers, and low-flying planes.

Nicklaus addresses his ball and never looks up. He watches the ball intently, gripping his club tight. The sign sways wildly, creaking like mad. But Nicklaus starts his swing. As the club reaches the top of the backswing, there is the loudest screech of all from the gyrating sign. The crowd grimaces as Nicklaus continues to swing and the sign continues to squeal. Around comes the clubhead, and far and true down the fairway sails the ball.

Someone asks Nicklaus if he was bothered by the racket. "I didn't hear anything," he says.

"You know," says Deane Beman, the P.G.A. commissioner, "that's what sets Jack Nicklaus apart from everyone else. His concentration. He has complete control over his emotions, his game, and his life."

The famed Nicklaus aptitude for concentration began

to make itself known in 1959 when he won the United States Amateur championship. He was just nineteen years old. The next year he finished second in the United States Open, the world's most prestigious tournament. In 1961 he won the amateur title again.

Turning professional, Nicklaus went on to win the Open five times, the Masters five times, the British Open three times, and the P.G.A. championship four times. That adds up to nineteen major victories, far more than any other golfer. Bobby Jones had thirteen, and Walter Hagen eleven, while Ben Hogan and Gary Player totaled nine and Arnold Palmer eight. Nicklaus had won sixty-nine tour events up to the time this was written. Moneywise, he had totaled over $4 million in purses. No one else has reached the $2-million mark.

Naturally, it took more than thought control to accomplish all that. Nicklaus was a prodigy from the start, an ungainly-looking one at that, though, as he was pudgy, heavy-legged, and swung as if off balance. However, the result is what counted, and Nicklaus seemed to be able to put it all back together at the moment the club impacted with the ball.

The result: thunderous drives that averaged 285 yards and many that surpassed 300 yards. At 5 feet 11½ inches and about 200 pounds, he usually intimidated his youthful opposition with his first swing. As he himself admits: "I could never believe that there was any other player better than I. I had a certain cockiness in me that showed, I guess."

Nobody parlayed that assurance into a winner any better. The first round of golf that he shot—at the age of ten—he racked up a 51 for nine holes. But he might not have been a champion golfer at all—he was very good in basketball and football in high school—if his father hadn't injured an ankle one day.

Advised by his doctor that he had to walk two hours a

day to strengthen his leg, Charles Nicklaus decided to take up golf instead of just strolling. Jack kept his father company, and before long, he was trying out the game himself.

One afternoon his father sent a long drive about 260 yards down the fairway. Turning to his son, who was twelve at the time, he said half-kiddingly, "Beat that and I'll buy you a Cadillac." You can guess the rest. Jack stepped up to his ball, studied it in his even then, serious, intense manner, and drove it 290 yards. Though he didn't get the Cadillac, his destiny was set that day.

Confidence never hurt Nicklaus, either as a boy or as a man. "Ego isn't a flaw with champions, it's an attribute," asserted one Nicklaus admirer. "It's what helped make Jack Nicklaus the world's premier golfer."

And Nicklaus has admitted: "People expect me to win, and I expect to win. If I didn't, I'd feel like a bum."

Later, he said he was ashamed of having made that remark, blaming it mostly on how easily he used to win in his youth. "Now that I think back on it," he said, "I'd say that it was a ridiculous assumption—false and utterly idiotic."

Soon after he outdrove his father, young Jack was put under the tutelage of Jack Grout, a local pro in Columbus, Ohio, where Nicklaus grew up. Here's how Grout "discovered" him:

"I was playing at the Scioto Country Club and had just smoked a good one off the tee at No. 16 over the hill in the fairway. Then I hit onto the green with a 7-iron. Just after I started walking toward the green, a ball came whizzing by me. I looked around and couldn't see anyone. Pretty soon here comes little Jack, Charlie Nicklaus's son, playing all by himself. That was his drive. I knew right then this kid was something."

Grout, as some teachers might, never tried to harness or cut back on young Nicklaus's phenomenal power. He never let him play anything but the back of the tees, explaining: "Jack can get control later. I tried to impress upon him what he might face if he became a great player, so I let him practice in the rain, even in a fifty-mile-an-hour gale. And he played 36 holes no matter what. That's where he developed his fierce determination, I'm sure."

With Grout guiding him and his father financing him, Nicklaus developed his already amazing skills. He probably would have succeeded at whatever sport he picked. He was good at everything he tried.

"When he told me he wanted to play football in junior high," said his father, "I told him he wasn't fast enough. He didn't say anything more, but I'd forgotten how determined he could be. Later that year, he came home to dinner and casually asked if I was going to the track meet that night.

"I said, 'Why should I?' and he said, 'Because I'm running.' That night, competing against older boys, Jack won the 100-yard and 220-yard dashes, anchored the winning 880-yard relay team, placed second in the high jump and broad jump. Then he comes home, hands me the ribbons he'd won and says: 'Do you think I'm fast enough for football now?' "

At Upper Arlington High School, Jack became a varsity baseball catcher and a four-year letterman in basketball. Scholarships poured in from colleges. Jack picked the one nearest home, Ohio State, even though he didn't get a scholarship.

At Ohio State, Jack Nicklaus tuned his golf game even more and won everything in sight. He became the youngest amateur champion in fifty years, was named to the Walker Cup squad and married his college sweetheart, Barbara. When he realized that he could make more money on a golf course than in the insurance business, or any other business, he left college and became a pro.

However, he credited his final year as an Ohio State amateur for paving the way. Still nineteen, he was chosen for the Walker Cup team, a team of amateurs that competed against a team of British amateurs. He won both his matches and helped the American squad win.

"Simply being selected gave me new confidence in my-

141

self," he said. "Then it made me demand even more of myself in future tournaments, which made me play better than I ever had. The way it seems to me, in golf you're always breaking a barrier. When you bust it, you set yourself a little higher barrier and try to break that one."

The Walker Cup experience proved to be the springboard from which Nicklaus went on to establish one of the most impressive amateur records of all time. He was defeated only once in thirty matches. He won the North and South championship, added the Grand Challenge Cup at Sandwich, England, and retained his Trans-Mississippi title. Playing with the professionals on their summer tour, he was the top amateur in three open tournaments. After several other victories, he placed second to Palmer in the U.S. Open, with a score of 272, the lowest ever shot by an amateur in that tournament.

He turned pro in 1961 and in the next year he finished in a tie with Palmer for the championship of the 62nd U.S. Open at Oakmont Country Club in Pennsylvania. In the 18-hole playoff, he defeated Palmer, 71 to 74, to become the youngest Open champion since Bobby Jones, who also won the 1923 Open at twenty-one.

If there hadn't been worldwide attention on this phenomenal young golfer, there was now. He began to be compared with the flamboyant Palmer, and many of Palmer's fans began resenting the upstart who had challenged their hero. Sensing the public attitude, Nicklaus reached inside himself and strove even harder for golfing perfection.

The barriers began falling like dominoes once Nicklaus began parlaying the confidence he already had with his tremendous willpower. The golf world had several gods, among them Jones, who mastered the game; Walter Hagen, who had made the professional game respectable; Ben Hogan, who proved it was possible to overcome adversity, and Palmer, whose golf charisma raised golf to new heights of popularity. Nicklaus outdid these gods, and then some.

Nicklaus broke Jones's magnificent records. He left Hagen's consistency in the lurch. He captured the U.S. Open on the same course Jones and Hogan had won, but his 269 bettered Hogan's 72-hole score by a record 18 shots. And then he caught popular Palmer by beating him head to head in the Open, the Masters, and the P.G.A.

"Nicklaus is so far superior to the rest of us," exclaimed one veteran of the tour, "that we might as well give him four shots every round. And that includes everyone, right up to and including Palmer."

Though Palmer didn't gleefully give up his crown to Nicklaus, he admitted, "Jack has an understanding of the game of golf that many don't have at the age of thirty-five."

Gene Sarazen, another of golf's earlier superstars, added: "I never thought anyone would ever put Hogan in the shadows, but Nicklaus did. He has the remarkable combination of power and finesse, and he is one of the smartest guys ever to walk the fairways. And he has been an extraordinary leader. What more is there to say? Jack Nicklaus is the greatest competitor of them all."

Ask Mr. Nicklaus, and he will agree that it takes more than just hitting the ball a mile to become No. 1. "Where's the fun, where's the challenge in just beating at the ball?" he says. "Any idiot can do that, and if he's strong enough, he'll score well. That's not what golf's about, though.

"It's a thinking man's game."

Nicklaus, in fact, regards length off the tee as one of the two worst characteristics of modern golf. (The other has to do with gigantic greens.) He says: "Power is overemphasized to a point where it's become totally out of proportion to the basic nature and enjoyment of the game. Golf is a game of precision, not strength."

Nicklaus credits that insight for a lot of his success. "I used to look at a bunker 260 yards away and hit the ball over it," he said. "Now, I aim to avoid it. That's life, and that's golf."

Managing a golf course is the key, he asserts. And so do others. "Nicklaus and Hogan," said Tom Watson, the newest tour star to challenge Nicklaus's throne, "they manage the courses so well, they don't let the courses manage them. I've learned that from them. I don't use my driver off the tee all the time now. I don't go for the pin all the time. That's why I've had some good years."

At the Masters, Nicklaus is usually king, and here's why: He takes careful notes on the course before every tournament. He marks down certain landmarks on each hole and then paces off their distance from the green. Then he memorizes them so well he can rattle them off like an auctioneer.

"First hole—tree on the right 154 yards to the front of the green, 180 to the back. Second hole—last ridge in the fairway 222 yards to the front of the green, 250 to the back. Manhole cover in center of the fairway 60 yards from the front. To carry the left bunker 71 yards, right bunker 74 yards. To keep from going over the green on the left 81 yards, on the right 84 yards. Third hole—front edge of the fairway trap 95 yards from front of green, 125 to the back."

Explains Nicklaus: "If you look at the P.G.A. figures, you'll see that the guy with the best average is usually less than a stroke under the guy back in thirtieth place. So you're talking about a fifth of a stroke a day between winning and thirtieth, and, by jiminy, you can't tell me there's that much difference in our swings. The difference is something else. It just might be in studious preparation."

Another edge might be his personality—steadfast. "I almost never get mad on a golf course," he says. "Actually, I smile a lot inside, but my face isn't built for smiles."

If anything, Nicklaus's powerful swing is probably not as graceful as a Jones's or a Snead's, and he'll be the first to admit it. "That's not the point," he begins. "The significant thing about my swing is that I understand it, so that if I take it apart, I can put it back together again. A lot of players on the tour don't know what to do about it when something goes wrong with their swing. Arnold Palmer knows, and I think I know pretty well, too."

Nicklaus also has stubby fingers, which give him a smaller grip and thus a more potential source for loss of control. That is one reason why it is common to see Nicklaus bent over a ball for so long a time; he looks frozen. Actually, he is concentrating, playing the stroke through in his mind before committing himself to its execution. His deliberate style on the greens makes his opponents uneasy. He will stand nervelessly over a putt more than thirty seconds sometimes, eyes focusing alternately on the ball, then the hole, as many as nine times.

"Other players are likely to sink their long putts in one tournament," Nicklaus says, "then miss some short ones in another. I won't make the long ones, but I won't three-putt much, either."

Controlling your emotions, Nicklaus thinks, helps you win. "Choking," he says, "is when you can't control your emotions. We all choke a bit. Emotions sometimes help you win, but sometimes you can't control them and you lose."

One old pro made the best observation of Nicklaus's control over his emotions that anyone has: "Nicklaus may play slowly, and he may be overdeliberate, but I've noticed one thing: He doesn't seem to have to hit the ball as often as those other fellows."

One biographer of Nicklaus described his tremendous concentration by writing: "Once he walks off the eighteenth green, Nicklaus is so relaxed that he could probably fall asleep at a New Year's Eve party. On the course, he is a study in utter concentration: cold, phlegmatic, withdrawn.

"Unlike the jovial, wisecracking Palmer, he often goes through an entire round without speaking a word. On the Merion course, Nicklaus was attempting a 20-foot birdie putt in the rain and wind. As he addressed the ball, a gust blew his cap off. He never paused, calmly stroked the ball into the hole."

Nicklaus often calls this aspect of golf "attitude." He

145

thinks he has developed a better attitude toward winning major championships because he truly believes they are easier to win. This is his explanation:

"Major championships are played on tougher courses, which eliminates a lot of people. Therefore, you really have a smaller field to beat than in a regular tournament. Also, a major championship is a battle of nerves. What I mean is there aren't that many players who can actually visualize themselves winning. They're defeated from the start. Therefore, those of us who think we *can* win, have fewer people to beat.

"Winning breeds more winning," he says. "You learn how to win by winning. As long as I'm prepared, mentally and physically, I always expect to win."

Since there is always a bit of luck in any round of golf, Nicklaus's skill and control usually take care of that, and his mental acuity completes the rest. It is a very tough combination to beat.

As a result, success has come more readily and easily to Nicklaus than to any other golfer in history. Most of the great players have had to serve a long, often cruelly hard apprenticeship in the ways of life and their craft. Not Nicklaus, who was astonishingly good almost from the first year he touched a club.

He was seemingly born with those golfing skills. Where he gained the unwavering desire to win, the urge to establish such a brilliant record, and such astonishing determination is the scintillating question. Some of his peers claim this foundation rose out of an exceptional character.

"He has that impregnable confidence," says one golfer, "that is an almost overpowering belief in himself. I have never seen the likes of it in any other athlete. Faith in one's ability is perhaps the greatest single gift a golfer can have. He believes in Nicklaus first, and nothing seems to penetrate this armor."

The analysis continues: "When Nicklaus wins, his reaction is that of confident expectation. That is, his attitude betrays nothing of surprise or relief, merely a calm assumption that the fitness of things has been properly observed. He is strangely unexcitable and, in many respects, almost inhumanly so."

Nicklaus's extraordinary assurance has always been evident to those around him. His directness can be disconcerting, though, especially to those who don't know him well. It is disturbing until one realizes that however critical or insensitive a Nicklaus remark may be, it is not intended to hurt or displease. It is the product of a mind that always reacts honestly.

This may be true of the really great performers. Since they are ever seeking perfection, they cannot indulge themselves in such luxuries as comforting flattery. Their unrelenting honesty may destroy, but in the end helps create their own strength.

Speaking of perfection, Nicklaus said: "In terms of execution, I feel the nearest I've ever got to the goals I've set myself is 75 percent. One aspect of my personality that has at times helped my career, and at other times brought me a lot of heartache, is my desire for perfection. I hate to do anything less well than I believe it can be done. And most of all, I hate to play golf less well than I think it can be played.

"Of course, I have never played golf perfectly. But that doesn't mean to say I won't go on trying to for as long as I feel I have some chance of meeting that goal. How would I define perfection in golf? What to me would represent a flawless performance?

"If I could achieve 100 percent in everything—on a par-72 course, I would shoot birdies on the fourteen par-3 and par-4 holes, and eagles on the four par-5 holes. That would give me an 18-hole score of 50, and four such rounds in a 72-hole tournament would be 200.

"As I see it, three elements are involved in playing per-

147

fect golf. First, I would have to have achieved 100 percent analytical objectivity—recognized the ideal shot for each situation. Second, having recognized the perfect shot, I would have to have resolved to play it—no compromises. Third, having recognized and resolved to play the perfect shot, I would have to have executed it perfectly—no technical hitches."

If all of this sounds like a wild daydream, you just don't know Jack Nicklaus.

# 12

# JIMMY CONNORS

## Hate Plus Talent Equals Success

Name the most successful male tennis players of this era, and more often than not, Jimmy Connors will either head the list or be next in line. Name the most controversial players in the sport, and Jimmy Connors more than likely will head that list, too. What makes this dual combination irresistibly intriguing is the fact that Jimmy Connors could not have accomplished one without the other.

The portrait of Connors the tennis player is a brilliant study in near-100-percent efficiency. Comparatively small at 5 feet 10 inches and 150 pounds, with shoulders that seem disproportionate to a sunken chest, strong but non-muscular legs and lean arms, Connors plays a ferocious type of game by hurling his whole body into nearly every shot. Not just an arm and two legs like most of us, but both arms, the torso, shoulders, neck and legs. Accompanied with such violence, the force carries him off the ground while in the act of stroking the ball.

There is fury in Connors's game, expressed openly by his animal-like grunts on every shot, gasps of breath while stretching for an overhead or serve, squeals from his turbulent footwork and, finally, the loud metallic "pow!" of the ball as it impacts against his trampoline-like steel racquet.

Virtually every ball is propelled with all the might Connors's body can muster, and every stroke is explosively powerful. There is no in-between, whether off the forehand, the two-handed backhand, the overhead smash, or putaway volley at the net. The ball comes blasting across the net at an incredible pace, crashing like an artillery shell against an opponent's racquet.

Besides the power delivered from a left-handed base, Connors possesses agility, speed, anticipation, and grace, all of which disguise his game and make his superhuman efforts look almost nonchalant. He moves like a ballet dancer, then stalks and kills with the apparent ease of a panther.

However, at the very same time Connors is devouring

151

an opponent, he is also expressing his uninhibited delight (or is it insecurity?) in just as open a manner. He enjoys mugging on court, in making faces, in imitating a belly dancer with a bump and grind, in sticking out his tongue, in shouting at an official, in laughing out loud (even at himself), in making obscene gestures, in wisecracking, in behaving like a brat, and in generally attempting to communicate with anyone within earshot.

When you've seen a Connors match, you feel you have witnessed a three-dimensional performance. It's not just tennis, but a drama and a comedy of psychological proportions. Watching Connors at play is to become engaged to him in some unforgettable way. He can blister an opponent, antagonize an audience, and drain himself all at the same time. Throughout, he appears to enjoy the whole show.

Relying on some inner turbulence to bring his aggressive game to full fruition, Connors seems to thrive on a give-and-take atmosphere of hatred. He becomes the villain, and everyone else is the good guy. That feeling seems to buoy him and constantly raise him to great deeds. Not surprisingly, he is the first to admit it, saying:

"I'm a different person when I'm on the court. I'm an animal, and I'm proud of it."

Animal, showoff, killer, or whatever, Connors's record speaks for itself. No one since Fred Perry in the '30s had captured three United States men's singles championships until Connors did in 1974, '76, and '78. He was the first American player since Bill Tilden in the '20s to reach five straight U.S. championship finals.

However, the aspect that sets Connors apart from anybody else and proves he is one of the most remarkable players ever is his adaptability: He won his first U.S. Open on grass, his second Open on clay (Har-Tru), and his third on asphalt (rubberized), three entirely different surfaces, each of which requires tremendous adjustments in style, strategy, and timing.

Connors may have achieved his greatest fame in 1974, when he swept the Australian, Wimbledon, and U.S. championships and won 99 of 103 matches. He might have completed the rare Grand Slam of tennis, but he was barred from the French Open because he had participated in World Team Tennis.

Said Connors: "One thing I know, they'll be talking about 1974 when I'm six feet under. I don't know if anybody can hit a tennis ball better than I did that year."

When he lost all those championships in the finals the following year, Connors considered it his all-time low and said: "Being No. 2 is like being No. 200. It's the same."

Modesty has never been one of Connors's strong points. His cockiness may make you smile or laugh, but it also brings out the worst reactions, too, like disgust or even hatred.

"I don't think anybody will ever play the game like I do," Connors has said. "I push myself to the point of no return. When I hit a ball, my whole body is in the air, twisting and turning, flying. I can't hold back. I play every point like I was down match-point. But that's when I play my best."

Other players describe what it's like facing Connors. Brian Gottfried said: "When Jimmy's playing his game, he just intimidates you. He can make you look like a fool, running from side to side. If he's not always the best player in the world, he is certainly the most exciting."

Dick Stockton compared playing Connors to fighting Joe Frazier, the former world heavyweight champion, saying: "He's always boring in on you, hitting you with everything he's got and never easing up."

Such statements reveal an important facet of Connors's character. To hit out all of the time requires tremendous confidence in your own ability, which Connors seems to have. That kind of faith can only be borne out by true dedication, outstanding skill, hard conditioning, and fierce concentration.

Pancho Segura, his coach, asserted, "Jimmy is the

153

closest thing you'll see to a complete player. He can do everything. He is a master of the approach shot, the top-spin lob, and overhead smash, but the keys to his game are his groundstrokes and volleys. I teach him to never let a ball come to you; charge it."

That is exactly what Connors does. He takes the ball almost as soon as it starts its upward rise from the surface. Then he leans into it and powders it on a flat trajectory across the net. His pace is considered the fastest on a consistent basis of any player. And when he senses the kill, Connors moves to the net where he can finish off the play in one dynamite swing.

"I don't like the ball," says Connors with a twinkle in his eye. "I don't like that little thing coming back over the net. So my first instinct is to hit the hell out of the ball."

When Connors is not sticking to the task of hitting the hell out of the ball, however, he can be found antagonizing the hell out of people. He has lots of irritating antics. For one, his on-court behavior often goes beyond pure gamesmanship. He'll blow on his hand for what seems an interminable length of time while getting ready to serve. He'll bounce the ball over and over until his opponent stalks off in a huff.

Sometimes when he hits a winner, Connors will turn his back on his opponent with a calculated flourish to rub it in. But when his opponent hits a winner near the line, Connors can act just the opposite. He'll glare at the linesman. He'll shout expletives. He'll joust orally with spectators in the stands.

It's when he takes on the crowd that Connors usually behaves his worst. One year he even leaped into the stands to go after a boisterous fan. He will hurl back obscenity after obscenity, driving spectators into a furor. ("I must have come out of the womb arrogant," Connors says, "because I've always walked and acted the same way.")

Though it made exciting reading in the newspapers and no doubt attracted more people to the matches, the results of Connor's brashness afforded him the permanent label of "punk" with many observers. He mellowed, of course, in his later years, overcoming many of his offensive and vulgar displays, but he has not been able to eradicate that image of old.

Connors explained it frankly by saying, "I can't look back. I can take the heat. Life is like tennis or business or anything else. You have to get hit in the mouth a few times before you learn.

"So I'm a jerk. Everybody knows that. I can't change on the court. I was branded when I was sixteen before I ever really did anything big in tennis. But I'm not knocking it, for people are buying tickets. I'm still happy with the way I am. I like my image."

That may be the most revealing part of Jimmy Connors's character. It seems he has to be disliked in order to win. To become unpopular, he intentionally puts everyone off until he stands alone against the world. This system works as long as Connors keeps winning. The public can accept almost anything, it appears, if it's accompanied by excellence. Just call it charisma and you can get away with it. It's the name of the celebrity game.

Chris Evert Lloyd, the former women's tennis champion who was engaged to Connors and knew him as well as anyone, said: "He's two completely different people on and off the court. The madder he gets, the better he plays. Jimmy can't beat someone he likes. He has to hate the person he's playing."

Connors is the first to agree with this, saying that he thrives on antagonism. "I like to have fans against me," he has said. "I want to do everything I can to get them against me more. When they're yelling at me, I really get into the match. I guess what I'm trying to do is show them that no matter how much they hate me, they have to respect the way I play."

Connors believes that "people pay to see me get beaten."

If that was all it was about, it could be understood, perhaps. But when Connors allows his control to get away from him and lets the tension and his quivering nerves produce emotional tantrums, it turns him not only into a villain, but also a despised and somewhat sick specimen.

Connors explains it this way: "Well, I'm hot and I'm thirsty. I'm tired and I hear things yelled at me, and I crack. I'm so intense and highly strung, I sometimes don't know what I'm doing. Afterward, I even have to laugh at myself."

A few years ago in the U.S. Open at Forest Hills, Connors was engaged in a tense match with Corrado Barazzutti of Italy. Connors hit a winner down the line that the Italian protested, asking that the linesman who called it good come out and check the ball mark. Before he could, though, Connors raced around the net and erased the mark with his shoe. Then he sneaked back to his side, smiling devilishly.

He was severely reprimanded by the umpire and drew boos and catcalls from the crowd. "I don't know why I did that," Connors said later. "I don't think you'll ever see anything like that again."

Nevertheless, Connors did not apologize for that incident and has not been known to issue apologies for any of his indiscreet actions. He also owns a reputation of being a terrible loser, while some players have called him the loneliest player on the whole tour.

What causes a man to become such a winner on the court and such a loser off it? As mentioned at the outset, the reasons are intertwined and feed off each other. They were formed long ago, probably before Connors was born. An examination of Connor's early life, his upbringing, his family relationships, and his boyhood training reveal some answers.

Connors has hinted at it when he said: "I'm not here to please the players or the press. And not the fans, either. It's the way I was brought up, with my mom and grandmom. Everywhere we went, it was the three of us. Nobody told me to do anything but them. And I listened. They were the only two people I ever listened to. Even now, you know, I listen to my mom."

Though he is not one to talk about his private life, the facts of his early years have emerged. We know how he was raised by two women, how his father virtually remained out of his life and how he was incessantly driven toward becoming a tennis champion by his mother and grandmother. We are aware of how he had to sacrifice the proms, the parties, the tree-climbing, the football, and basketball games, the intimate relations with girls and boys and many of the other social practices teenagers normally pursue.

Jimmy Connors, we've learned, became the sole focus of his mother and grandmother, whom he called "two-mom," to the exclusion of everything else. His older brother, Johnny, was deemed not to have the "guts" to become a star, so Jimmy received all their attention. Psychologists have called his lack of a real relationship with his father one of the most pertinent shapers of his character.

Gloria Connors, his mother, could undertake to teach Jimmy the finer points of tennis because she was a tennis instructor, as was her mother. She had always dreamed of being a tennis star, traveling in elite company all over the world, and when she married, that dream was shattered. So she turned her ambition on her son.

From the age of two, Jimmy began getting instruction in the game. Constantly under the scrutiny of his mom and two-mom, he was coached and molded and guarded and taught, while nearly everything else was discarded. Tennis became life.

Explained Gloria Connors: "My mother started teaching me at five. I started Jimmy at two. Jimmy's grandmother forgot more about tennis than most pros claim to know. She really made a study of the game. Yes, Jimmy really had two moms. I was No. 1 mom, and my mother was No. 2 mom.

"Yes, we were very close, best friends, really. I did

**157**

nothing for twenty-three years but work for Jimmy. I taught him how to swim and I taught him how to play tennis. To me, sports is the answer to anything."

Jimmy ended up playing tournament tennis when he was seven and gained a national ranking when he was twelve. Even then, when a famous tennis coach wanted to take Jimmy under his wing and put him in his group, Mrs. Connors declined, saying she felt just as qualified as anyone to teach her son tennis.

Even today, Mrs. Connors is proud to point out that she and her mother were the only women ever to have developed a men's champion. There were other major influences, though, and one of the biggest outside helpers was Segura, who was brought in specifically to make Connors "think like a man" on the court.

Until that day, however, Connor's future was shaped by his mothers. Not wishing to become part of the country-club life around St. Louis, where they lived, Jimmy's mother constantly imparted her philosopy to her son: "They're all out to get us." No wonder Jimmy Connors grew up not able to trust anyone but his mother.

Connors says: "She's my mom, you know, the one who creates you. She's my mom first and always will be. But she's my coach and my friend, too. Where would I be today if it hadn't been for her?"

There's the story of the day when Connors was sixteen and beat his mother for the first time in tennis. He seemed beside himself with embarrassment and came to the net full of apologies, saying: "Gee, Mom, that hurt. I didn't mean to do that."

His mother is supposed to have replied: "No, no, Jimmy, don't you know? This is one of the happiest days of my life." Five years later, Connors won Wimbledon.

"Yes, sir, Jimmy and I played every day of the year, every year," said Gloria. "And we played hard. I taught him to be a tiger. 'Get those tiger juices flowing!' I would yell. I even told him to try and knock the ball down my throat, and he learned to do this because he found out that if I had the chance, I would knock it down his. And then I would say, 'You see, Jimbo, you see what even your own mother will do to you on a tennis court?' "

Connors learned well. "No one's ever given me anything on the court," he said. "Maybe that's one reason I prefer singles. It's just me and him. When I win, I don't have to congratulate anyone. When I lose, I don't have to blame anyone."

So Connors became a tough guy on the court, glaring hard at opponents, flaunting tennis's traditional niceties, and acting truly as if it were he against the world, as he was taught.

"How long can he win on hate?" asked a player. "It's the way he was taught," said another, "and his nature."

Many people thought Connors had emerged from the womb when he became engaged to Chris Evert in an over-publicized romance. The alliance reached unbelievable heights when both Jimmy and Chris won Wimbledon titles in the same year, but then the "duet made in heaven" gradually collapsed as Connors returned home to live with his mother-coach.

"When Mom's with me, I've got it made both ways, my mom and my coach," he said. Later, she became his business adviser as well.

"As well as I know Jimmy," said Chris Evert, "a lot of times I don't know what goes on in his head. But if he still has me baffled, I know that he's still got himself baffled, too. Jimmy might know himself better if he would ever spend some time soul-searching. But he won't.

"He's always had to hate the men players to be at his best. But they don't hate *him* anymore. A lot of them have even come to like him. So he's got to find a new motivation, and that's going to be very hard for Jimmy."

One observer on the tour said: "Connors tried to become a good guy, but it didn't work. People weren't going to forget everything and suddenly accept him for the asking.

159

He still has no close friends, and his mother drove away most of the girls he was involved with."

When Arthur Ashe found a way to beat Connors in the final of the 1975 Wimbledon tournament, it proved another turning point. He started losing the big tourneys in the finals. Explained a player:

"Connors experienced something that happens to all top players. Someone beats you and then everyone thinks they can. Ashe changed things with his victory. He showed there was an effective strategy that could be used against him, and that gave everyone else more confidence."

Trying to improve his image, growing up, and losing some big matches could have sounded the death knell for Connors, who needs the killer instinct to survive. But then came the antidote for his problems—Bjorn Borg, the Swedish star who came along and beat Jimmy enough to claim the No. 1 ranking.

Said Segura: "You have to work hard to win. No one wins on three shots anymore. You have to run your rear off and it's hard for Jimbo because of all he's accomplished. Borg is the best thing that ever happened to him. He makes Jimbo work to prove he's still the best. He's making Jimbo a mean killer again."

The change was obvious after Borg ravaged Connors in a Wimbledon final, 6–4, 6–2, 6–2. Connors vowed revenge, stating: "I'll follow that sonofabitch to the ends of the earth. Every tournament he enters, I'll be waiting. Every time he turns around, he'll see my shadow across his face. I'm going to dog him because I know that what we do in the next few years is going to be remembered long after we're both gone."

Though Borg and Connors battled each other over and over, no final and clear victor emerged at first. Connors achieved his so-called revenge at the U.S. Open by beating Borg as badly as he had ever been beaten. It was the old Connors in action, with the clenching of the fists in the air and the veins in his neck popping out and those blood-curdling screams emitted after a winning shot.

Such is Connors's character: He can barely accept losing, and he cannot cope with having been beaten. In the final at the U.S. Open a year later, he was soundly defeated by Guillermo Vilas and ran out of the award-giving ceremony without even a goodbye.

"Running away like that is entirely in character," observed Arthur Ashe. "I hope you didn't expect anything else from him."

Added Bill Riordan, his former manager: "He has no one to tell him what's right and what's wrong and he certainly doesn't know himself."

Yet, Connors still offers Borg a real challenge, and vice-versa. They have formed the classic rivalry, the quick-footed Swede with the big topspin ground strokes from the baseline against the power-hitting American whose shots travel deeper and faster than anybody else's.

"Connors plays differently than anyone else," noted John Newcombe, a former champion. "He's a lefty with a kick serve and a two-fisted backhand, and you don't see other lefties like that. And he hits a flat-out ball with incredible pace that takes some getting used to."

Added Segura: "Jimmy's grown physically and mentally over the years. He's still growing. He can outplay anybody on the courts today. He has tremendously quick reactions. He can play on any surface. The one I compare him with most is Rod Laver at his best."

What makes Connors a most admirable player in the game despite his psychological problems is this: He always gives everything he has to a game. Even on an off day, he is never lackluster. He can overcome his fears, he refuses to throw a match (as some players do when they're not at their best or become angry), and he offers no excuses for defeat.

This is how Connors describes his style: "I was taught that lines were there to be hit. I'd rather hit a ball long than into the net any day. I go for winners. I take chances, even when I don't have to. I don't like to chicken out.

"I play it safe once in a while, but then I realize right away that I'm playing like a chicken when I should be going for the line. I always play my game. I always will. Till death do us part."

This is a point of pride on Connors's part. He says it again and again: "It isn't me if I don't play the way my mom taught me. My mom gave me my game, and she taught me one way, that lines were made to be hit.

"My mom and my grandma were the only ones who ever touched my game, and they taught me to play one way. There's no other way."